Back to the Source

*Cultivating Inner Peace
in a Technology-Driven World*

HAILEY JORDAN YATROS

Love yourself fully! xoxo Hailey

Copyright © 2016 Hailey Jordan Yatros

Books may be ordered through booksellers or by visiting:

www.createspace.com
www.amazon.com
www.haileyyatros.com

The author of this book does not dispense medical advice or prescribe the use of any technique as a form of treatment for physical, emotional, or medical problems without the advice of a physician, either directly or indirectly. The intent of the author is only to offer information of a general nature to help you in your quest for emotional and spiritual well-being. In the event you use any of the information in this book for yourself, which is your constitutional right, the author and the publisher assume no responsibility for your actions.

Printed in the United States of America.

Front Cover Design by Amanda Walker
Edited by Laura McMurry
Back Cover Photo by Beech Photography

ISBN-10: 0692790268
ISBN-13: 978-0692790267

*Dedicated to those (young and old)
that ache to feel peace and contentment in an
ever-changing, competitive, technology-driven world.*

PRAISE FOR THE BOOK

"*Back to the Source* captured my attention from the first paragraph. I thoroughly enjoyed this book and learned several things along the way. Some I knew but never practiced; some I hadn't even thought of, and other things that just make so much sense. The writing was conversational and comfortable. Hailey Jordan Yatros is someone to watch. She's just getting warmed up." – Sandy Richards, Award-Winning Author of *A Far Cry … From Home: A Mother's Journey of Love, Loss, and Healing…Through the Eyes of an Angel*

"Just reading this book surreptitiously brings the reader back to their Source; it has all the tools you need to begin the journey. This book is very much like the book, *The Untethered Soul* for this generation!" – Denise L. Brooks PsyD, L.P. Owner of *Stepping Stones Wellness Center*

"For those of you searching for a way back to your truest Self, this book is for you! Hailey takes you on a journey to the roots of who you really are. *Back to the Source* will help you reach your fullest potential in Love, acceptance, and growth. Take the time to read this book carefully and absorb each lesson it has to offer." – Kay Beech, Owner and Founder of *Beech Photography*

What is Inner Peace?

Inner peace is the gentle reassurance that everything is going to be *okay*. Your life, your future, and your soul are at rest. It's a calming confidence you carry, no matter what you're facing.

Although you may not be certain of what's to come, you can be certain of what is inside of yourself.

CONTENTS

Back to the Source

Cultivating Inner Peace
in a Technology-Driven World

PART 1
Back To The Basics

"A bird sitting on a tree is never afraid of the branch breaking because her trust is not in the branch but on her own wings."
-Anonymous

I was *drowning* in anxiety for years. I'd come home from work – exhausted. Open my email, still hundreds left unanswered. Cry in the parking lot of my meaningless jobs because I didn't want to go in, I didn't want to be there, I wanted bigger things for my life. But I didn't want to wait for it. No one could ever tell that I was constantly fearful, wherever I went. Ignoring my phone messages became normality because I just didn't have the energy or capability of answering the question, "How are you?" I would gather up every last ounce of energy I had to heat up a meal, crawl back into my bed and hide from the world. Another day would pass and still I had the ever-present feeling that I hadn't done enough, that *I* wasn't enough. Morning came and the cycle would repeat.

I don't think we talk about it enough; how growing up in your twenties is unbelievably hard, unbearable at times. Everything seems like life or death, you are supposed to know what decisions to make and be able to plan for the future. Nothing is certain or steady in your early years; always adjusting, moving from place to place … trying to find stable ground in a shaky world.

Could it possibly be even harder nowadays living in a digital era that is shaped by technology and urgency? Maybe it's more difficult for *anyone* to find an inner calmness in a culture full of immediate demands and unpredictability. I would also argue that perhaps we are currently living in some of the most uncertain and changeable times yet. It has trickled into all generations today, not just the younger generation. And it is continuing; the upcoming generation is called Digital Natives. Is anything truly certain anyway? All I know is that if we don't know how to direct and take responsibility of our own lives, we will continue to hide behind our false fear and become overtaken by it.

This is not a book about how to eliminate technology from our lives, or limit the use of our cellphones, or even about spending less time on the Internet. It goes much deeper than that. It's about creating an unshakeable internal world so that *nothing* can disturb your peace. Although life gets hard, messy, and impulsive (as it always does) we can be internally equipped to handle it and rise above our current circumstances.

I've heard it said that only five per cent of the human spirit is used to its fullest potential. *Five per cent.* What about the other 95 per cent? People use expressions such as "that's just the way I am," not knowing that they could be so much more. What if what we're facing for this period of our lives isn't all that there is? What could happen if we decided to see beyond our current situations and limitations? How well have you navigated in today's times, with everything moving and changing at an unimaginable pace?

Our existence is full of unanswered questions, mysteries and possibilities. In order to fully understand and consider these questions, we need to get back to their origination.

Answers can only be found when we know the right questions to ask. So often things are moving so quickly that we get caught up in our daily rituals and routines and we don't even *know* something has to change. Day after day, year after year, we trudge ahead feeling like we cannot escape this uphill battle. It's as if we are sleep walking and unless something really bad happens, we're content with "just the way life is" and being "just the way we are."

I've been privileged to speak before many audiences during the past seven years and have coached several thousand individuals. After presenting, people often approach me asking for advice.

No matter who I talk to, or how their comments are framed, they all seem to have the same underlying question: "How can I find peace in an ever-changing society?" I was deeply moved to find a real, raw and truthful answer, as I was struggling with this as well, thus my mission began. (Ever seen a woman on a mission? Watch out!)

Little did I know that my life was about to change as a result of asking *this* question. I ended up on a hunt to *The Source*; the Source of who I am and how I could cultivate inner peace. Essentially, I figured out that my true Self and inner peace go hand-in-hand; when I neglected my true Self I lost my peace, and when I had peace it was because I was being my true Self. The Source is what I call the birthplace of our spirit and in reading you will discover what it truly means to *get back to the Source*.

As I started to explore, I realized that for as long as I can remember, I have been attracted to anything that symbolizes peace; a passing butterfly, a quiet fall evening, a trip to the mountain air, you name it. Everything in my soul longed for a feeling of calmness. Maybe it was because my childhood had been anything but peaceful. It may also have been because chaos filled so many areas of my life that I was desperate to find relief. I had searched for answers in books, in music, in companionship. What I finally came to understand was inner peace can only be enlivened inside of *myself* and that I couldn't do it alone.

We live in a world where there are constant invitations for distraction. There is always something competing for your attention. I don't think we actually realize how many times we are being pulled into multiple directions. The focus of your concentration and energy is very sacred and you must not allow it to overtake you. The Internet is not the only cause of this interference. All facets of technology have completely shifted and shaped our culture. Our society as a whole has changed the way we work, live and interact.

It's as if we live in a world where we are always eating yet never get full. It feels like gasping for air; trying to keep our heads above water. It's kind of like we can never get ahead. Can you relate to this feeling?

When I start to feel weighed down by problems,

caught up in anxiety of the future, or the turmoil of comparison, I think of these written words; *these truths are universal.* They transcend to all humankind. Which is why I have brought them to you, in this book. It is why I set out on a mission to write about it years ago. This book is a product of the discoveries I've made along the way.

Now, more than ever, each one of us craves peace. At the end of each day we want to feel a sense of accomplishment. But more than that, we want to truly know and believe with our hearts that everything is going to be okay. We want assurance that all of this, especially what is going on in our world today, will work itself out and that there is a higher purpose than what we see on the surface. We all desire this liberating feeling. It was, and is, my goal to bring this to all of you. And of course, I had to start with myself. Besides, I *desperately* needed to make a change in my own life, I had suffered for so long and my heart longed for freedom.

I wanted to know when I had done enough, and that I was on the right track. I wanted to answer that question about peace confidently whenever I was asked publicly. I wanted to feel fully alive and stop missing moments. I wanted to genuinely feel loved and worthy. I didn't want to anxiously pick my fingernails until they bled. I finally found resolutions – my answers. And although we will always be a work-in-progress, we can have the awareness of what to do in moments of feeling anxious and worried.

To be clear: This is NOT a book on balance. Balance is something I believe can rarely be achieved. I'm not sure it is even sustainable because everything in life ebbs and flows, there is rarely an equilibrium. This is a book about creating inner peace in the 21st century. A century defined by technology, distraction and urgent demands. It's about letting go of what is no longer serving us, and receiving new ideas and perspectives that could make all the difference. This journey is also about expanding and exploring the many qualities of Love.

Are you aware that many of the issues today's culture faces are restlessness, depression and anxiety? I'm not surprised. Nowadays, it's tough to distinguish between the urgent and the important, so our menial tasks fall under the category of urgent – which produces a constant fight-or-flight mindset. This makes us feel that we're always behind. The omnipresent feeling of struggle lingers constantly in the background. Also, being stuck in the fight-or-flight mode can pack on the pounds; it's what I call stress-weight.

Who wants that?

We'll overwhelm ourselves in angst and fear if we don't identify what *is* important. If we don't determine what's essential in our lives, the world will, and that's kind of a scary thing – don't you agree? As author and motivational speaker Jim Rohn said, *"If you don't design your own life plan, chances are you'll fall into someone else's plan. And guess what they have planned for you? Not much."* Quite frankly, people today actually *do* have a lot planned for you. They want all of your time, attention and focus to be on what's important to *them*.

What about you, my dear? What do you authentically, whole-heartedly, sincerely want? Is it peace? Inner confidence in who you really are? Success? More faith and less fear? More belief and less doubt? At the Source you will find you have everything you'll ever need.

PART 2
My Promise To You

Most uncertainty in our lives stems from not knowing what our path will entail or where to even begin. We fear that we might be wasting our time on what we are doing. When we're young, or just starting out in any endeavor, we tend to have a minimal track record for success, and therefore it's hard to believe in our abilities, skills and the purpose of our journeys. When we're older we think our time has passed and what our lives currently look like is all we've got. In either scenario, the question that unremittingly dwells within our minds is: "What is my calling?" In other words, "What is the purpose of my life?" Rightfully so, it is one of the most important questions we will ever consider in our lifetime.

Your calling is best described as a vocation; something you *need* to discover in your lifetime and that makes you feel absolutely complete. Essentially, it's the only job you *have* to do here, it'll keep nudging at you until it's discovered and used. It doesn't necessarily have to be your day job or even your work. Your calling is what you dedicate your life to doing, even if it never serves you financially. It's what makes your heart sing!

If you are struggling with what your calling might be, please don't stress about it. It's nothing you have to go out and find, rather it's something that you connect to; it's *already* inside of you. In reading, you may gather clues that could lead you further down the road to your vocation – just keep asking and looking. And don't worry, it could be *multiple* things, big or small. It could be as simple as checking on your neighbor periodically to make sure they're okay, or joining a community watch group.

Our sole job is to keep seeking within us – because it's there. We must ask the question: What satisfies my spirit? And then listen and keep listening and paying attention. Don't agonize over it, let it go and it will come. As Rumi said so beautifully, "What you seek is seeking you."

Your journey is unique. Guess what? I didn't always want to be a writer. It wasn't a majestic dream I've always had. I don't know how I got started or whatever made me want to start. All I knew was that I kept being led to share my thoughts on paper, and that something *changed inside of me* when I did. After spending hours or even ten minutes of writing in a day I would feel so alive, so excited and happy.

I'd walk outside my front door with my head held a little higher and pep in my step. I had a calmness in my heart like I had done good for the world. I kept on longing for that feeling, and so I kept on writing. Soon, I started to keep notepads and pencils everywhere I went, even in my car. My thoughts started to collect on sticky notes and placed in the most random places. It became an intricate part of me that I cherished. I gradually realized that writing was one of my callings. This is how it comes to us, though. Slowly, surely, and gently.

Most importantly, I had to *allow* it to come through me. Sometimes it starts with a whisper or just a little pull. So many of us ignore the signs and push it away. From reading this book you will explore simple techniques that will help you allow it to flow. If you pay attention to the feelings that surface from within, then you'll start to follow the hints – your emotions leave clues.

Contrary to what others may say, having a calling is not always convenient. It can seem like a lot to handle at times, especially if you are juggling numerous things. You want to only create, but you have a career/day job. You desire to develop your gifts further, but you have other responsibilities to attend to (you're a mother/father, a husband/wife, a daughter/son). I know, you have a lot of questions; a vocation brings peace and questions. It brings peace because you feel alive when you do it – so fulfilled. But it also brings questions because you want to be sure you're heading in the right direction. You want assurance that you're not just wasting your time. Should or shouldn't you turn it into a business? You crave certainty. Your calling can come with pressure.

Here is what I know. When I was a child I wanted to "save the world" – I aspired to be a hero. I'd see an aching heart, an animal that needed rescuing, an elderly person sitting alone, someone in need, and I would offer anything I could to help. Have you ever felt this way? Having large dreams is remarkable and a true treasure. Hold onto them.

Keep in mind, it's not about the size of your calling, it's about your saying "yes" to it. If you are taking care of yourself and doing what lights up your soul, you *are* being a hero – a hero to you. You are a part of a much bigger picture when you choose to follow your calling. Saying "no" to yourself is similar to dehydration – as if you're drying out – until you drink a glass of ice-cold water (your calling). Grabbing just a sip of water is soothing to the throat. That's how it will feel, even if it's at the smallest level; it'll be restorative to your heart. And by doing **that**, *you are helping the world.*

If you continue to discount what feeds your soul, you will thirst. It won't matter how fearful you become, or how insignificant you may feel, it's something that you *must* do. It could be painting, singing, beat-boxing, knitting, taking care of sick animals, dancing, gardening, anything. You can help the world by honoring you and what you exclusively give to others. You cannot demand an outcome of your calling; it needs to be for pure pleasure of the doing and being.

How do you feed your soul? How do you know when you are thirsty? What are you yearning *for*? What is your quest? Your inner spirit and highest Self want you to be true to who you are. It wants you to explore and express yourself to your full capability, and to live from every part of you, keeping nothing hidden. From the Source, your calling can emerge.

Your Comfort Zone
May Not Be So Comfy

Each one of us creates, works, loves and lives as far

as our comfort zones will allow. Comfort zones are known (and unknown) levels of familiarity in our lives that can inhibit us from trying new things, letting ourselves be fully seen and stretching to our highest capabilities. We end up building walls of security that keep us from exploring all the possibilities of our life. What we don't recognize, however, is that right beyond the wall we've built is where our true treasure lies. It's where our hidden potential sits, waiting to be discovered.

If we desire to get back to the Source of who we are, then we need to discover and assess our limits. How far do our comfort zones stretch? What are you willing to do? Not willing to do? We might just be pleasantly surprised at how far we'll go.

I'll be candid and share with you that it's not going to be easy. It will be unpredictable and messy, might even freak you out - but it must be done. The ideas I suggest in this book may test your comfort zone *and* your beliefs. May I ask that you simply try? I want the absolute best for you. Who knows? You may be surprised. Maybe the only comfort you will find will be *outside* of your zone.

The purpose of this book is to bring us back to the ultimate: To who we really are - to our *Source*. Amidst all the busyness, the worrying and the striving, my intention is to create a home; a place where we feel welcomed, protected and secure in ourselves. And, regardless of what is happening around us, *that we come to know a realm so much bigger within the own parameters of our hearts.*

Every day people undergo the inevitability of life. They can't find a job. They despise their work. They long for a companion. They are restricted by their bank balance. They are strained by unhealthy relationships. Circumstances like these affect how we handle ourselves and make decisions. What I am seeking to accomplish here is not to tell you how to get rid of your problems (wouldn't that be nice?), but to equip you to *handle* whatever it is you find yourself facing. This I know for sure: Our entire outer world is a direct reflection of our inner world. If you are all in, my promise to you is that you will learn how to take care of and cultivate your majestic and beautiful inner world.

My hope is that I make coming back to the Source as simple as possible, because in a world of overload and anxiety, we could use some simplicity in our lives.

When your find yourself struggling and asking, "What is the next right step for me?," how can you know which way to go? When you are stuck or drowning in anxiety/fear, what can ease your worries? If you're feeling unloved and unworthy, what truth can you stand upon? If you feel alone, or stuck, or lost, where can you seek connection and Love? At the Source you will find your answers. I have created a place for those who seek rest; to regain your inner peace and be centered in the deepest part of who you are. Trust that you are in the right place. Be open – and the rest will fall into place.

PART 3
Openness Is The Ultimate Freedom

Boxes were piled high in each corner of the apartment. A fully-packed U-Haul idled in the driveway. Friends were gathered to say their final goodbyes. My friend's next chapter had begun as she was about to enter a new city, new environment, new career, new friends, new everything.

Packed in those boxes in the corners of the apartment were pieces of the past: Her beliefs of who she was and the measure of bravery she *thought* she possessed.

You see, she had to step outside the world she knew so well to unlock what she was meant for, and it took every ounce of courage she had to do it. As soon as she started on her way, a tremendous amount of fear and guilt came flooding in, but she kept driving on the open road – she knew she had to do it. For once in her life she finally felt free.

Like my friend, every one of us knows our world so well. We know the beliefs and the safe restrictions we have created inside of ourselves. We know the secret places inside our hearts that we refuse to open. We are aware of the roads we refuse to travel down (or we ignore them). If you look closely, you can spot these restrictions in other people as well.

Have you ever tried telling somebody something and they reply, "Oh I already know that," or, "I've heard that before,"? It can be frustrating, right? Because we lose a moment to share and they lose a moment to be open. They close up. They are no longer accessible to seeing or discovering a new concept or perspective. It's almost as if their inner ear has been turned off.

Being open doesn't mean that we pretend we know nothing. On the contrary, when a person is open they are always full - full of wonder, curiosity and hope. A person who is open continually strengthens the relationship between learning and giving. They learn to give, and give to learn. It's a beautiful thing, being open, because the more wisdom we absorb, the more we can help and provide to others.

Positioning Yourself As A Blank Canvas

What I am suggesting, as we begin on this magnificent journey, is: Are you willing to be open? To truly strip away everything you "already know?" We are going to start over, if you will, just while reading this book. Can you sense the relief in, "Lets start over."? These words can give us such freedom. They provide us with the opportunity to create the type of person we want to be in the world. I think that is why hitting rock bottom is crucial for some people; they get to start again, from a renewed platform. Rock bottom can be a beautiful place.

Perhaps you had to start a project over from scratch, or start over in your career, or start over in a relationship, or completely start over in life. What did that feel like?

I remember writing an essay, a long and important one, and out of nowhere my computer crashed. Yes, *crashed*. I lost everything and I had to completely rewrite the whole thing. After I got over the shock and the "I can't believe this happened" feeling, it felt very humbling to start over. I was given another chance, a chance to re-write the story, potentially better than the first one.

The opportunity to start over can be refreshing, however it might not always feel that way at the time. Maybe for you it is dreadful, scary and exhausting. I know that for some it's incredibly tiresome. I had a friend who, for whatever reason, could not maintain a relationship. It was like a cycle – date for two years – break up – start over. After a few of these cycles he said to me, "I just hate starting over." He was growing weary and hopeless. Perhaps you can relate to this.

I remember quitting a job I knew it was time to leave, even though others thought I had it all (which made it even harder to do). At some point in our lives I think we *need* to get sick and tired of feeling miserable. We need to say, "Enough is enough," and move on. That's what had happened to me. I didn't want to fight anymore or feel captive to my own heart. It was difficult for me to make that decision, but finally, I did. I began again, and in fact that is how my book *The Millennial Makeover* was born; I made a choice to leave and BOOM! A new opportunity presented itself.

I think starting over allows you to pick up the pieces and regain your strength; to be transformed by your past and to march forward into the unknown. A good friend of mine always says, "We are climbing a mountain that has no top." It sounds wearisome, doesn't it? But it works. It truly works to start over. If you think about it, each day is another chance to begin again. Sometimes, life will even force us to do it and looking back, you might be able to see it was for the best.

By removing the self-inflicted obstacles in our way, we can open new doors for greater things to come. What if we gave *ourselves* permission to pack up, leave our baggage, and move forward? What if we gave ourselves clearance to start from scratch and reposition our lives; as if everything in our past was washed away? What if we had no inhibitions about ourselves? What if, just for a moment, we no longer said, "Oh that's not Me," or "I've never done that," or "Nope, not going to try that," or "I won't ever be able to do that." I used to say, "You should've done it this way, Hailey. You should've completed this instead. Wait, why did you just say *that*?" Shoulda. Coulda. Woulda.

What if you're not the shy person you think you are? And you are no longer the person that complains about things that are not changing? Instead, you are a strong creator; someone who puts his or her mind to something and sees it through to completion (even if it sucked).

Consider this: Who we are, is created only in *today*. So that all we know about ourselves is what we decide in this very moment. My friend always says, "Hailey, I just wish to be a nobody, knowing nothing, going nowhere." There is relief in a clean slate and beginning again. At some level, the past does serve us; we learn from our experiences and by doing so gain confidence to move ahead. We just can't stay in that place.

When beginning a project and plagued by fear, what if you said to yourself, "I've got this, let's go!," or "Sure! I'll try that; even if it's messy," or my personal favorite, "I don't know if this is going to work, but I'm going for it anyhow!" Think of how *free* we could be. What would it feel like for you to be free of your hang-ups, your insecurities and your worries? Free from the problems and obstacles that weigh you down; the guilt and shame that prevent you from moving forward. It is freeing just writing this down.

Can you put yourself into this mindset? I'm going to request that you continue reading from this space, and picture yourself as a blank canvas. From *this* mindset we are going to explore what it really means to live with inner peace. This is what it looks like to be sincerely open and that truly is the ultimate freedom.

Another way to think of this would be envisioning your life when you first came into this world as a newborn baby. You were innocent and pure. You had a blank slate and you didn't know anything. You didn't know what to do except to simply *be alive*. You couldn't distinguish the difference between lies and truth. You didn't know how to make decisions or deal with the pressure of not knowing. You just lived; you were taken care of – some way, some how. You didn't intellectualize, scrutinize, or make judgments about anything. What would it be like to live from nothing? This perspective causes peace in and of itself.

Let's pretend we know nothing. Can we just try this out? The empty. The nothingness. Without removing old junk, we can never put new stuff in.

Authenticity Is Real Power

When my inner being emanates harmony, I know I'm being authentic. When the day is done, if I've honored myself and given all I have to others, then I ultimately feel at peace. Let me give you an example: An article about me was published in a major magazine. I was excited; finally my big break had arrived – or so I thought... until I read it. I wasn't really a fan of the piece so I gave it no attention. Any publicity is good publicity, right? Well, soon multiple TV producers reached out to me to see if I'd be interested in doing a show. "I want to make you a star," said one of them. At first it was so exciting, I got caught up in the dream of it all. I'd always loved the camera, and this way I could touch more people more quickly. Before I knew it, four producers reached out to me in one month! It was flattering, but I know myself; I knew that I was being swept away in the energy of it all. I had to chill out and see if this was really a good move for me. I remember asking my closest friends, "What do you think I should do?" They all told me that deep down I knew what to do. So for a long time I was still about it. I prayed and meditated, and meditated and prayed some more. Having support from others is good, but sometimes your voice can be overshadowed and stifled by the opinions of others. Sometimes it's best to do it alone. We need to really learn to trust our intuition and pay attention to the feelings that arise from within - on our own. Self-awareness is the key to knowing which next right move is good for you. This is the epitome of inner peace. Because at the end of the day, it's you and you alone that has to make the decisions of your life.

I eventually came to the conclusion that something didn't sit right about it with me. I'm not really sure what it was; I couldn't put my finger on it, but I knew it wasn't the next right move for me – *at the time*. Humbly, I turned down the offers. I felt a sense of peace at the end of the day because I knew I was being authentic to who I really am. I was honoring myself at the deepest level regardless of the disappointment I was left with. It was the *feeling* that lead me to the *knowing*.

About a month later, I was asked by another production company in L.A. to move forth on a particular idea (it was quite different than what I was offered before). I can't disclose that information just yet, but I fell in love with this idea *instantly*.

I just smiled, and knew that I was being taken care of. I took it as a pat on the back, a job-well-done, because I listened to what *I* really wanted. I listened to my own request, to my inner voice – despite what others had desired from me. And now, I am currently in the process of being cast in a national television show centered around my coaching practice. I promise that if you can be still, wait for the true knowing that comes from within (instead of the one you manufacture), you'll be amazed at what is in store for you.

There are always options around us to be our

authentic selves: When we feel pain, express it; when it's time to move on, go; when the answer is no, then say no and allow the other person to stand in the disappointment.

You have instincts like these all the time. You have a strong intuition that is always communicating with you – we need only to listen and be aware. I've learned that only hearing your intuition isn't the hard part. What takes true courage is doing what it's asking of us.

Later in this book we explore what it looks and feels like to make decisions based upon our internal compass. During this process you may dance between the struggle of living how you want to, yet not upsetting anyone in the process. But the truth is that when we take ownership of this vehicle – this vehicle being our body/mind/spirit/life – then *we* are the drivers. We will always upset *someone*. Every so often we will take a side trip and end up where we didn't think we'd ever be (wrong relationship, career, or lifestyle), but ultimately we need to be chauffeurs of our own life. At times, that requires us to pass by a street or take "the road less traveled." It will upset some people, but our hearts know what is good for us and what we should steer clear from. We need only to listen, and then have the bravery to do what it asks.

When you decide to make this shift, to stand by your own truth, you will come up against giants. Do not be fooled. Armies of negative ogres and barriers remain on the road ahead. I am a tiny 4'11 and practically everyone I come into contact with literally looks down on me. Talk about insecurity. I do know what it's like to feel small, and not just metaphorically. But I also know that I am not my body. I have a heart as big as the universe, a deep commitment to my life's message and a strong craving to be grounded in the truth of who I am. I'd rather do things afraid than not do things *because* I am afraid. Instead, I'll allow God to use my smallness for His greatness.

Inner peace is the gentle reassurance that everything is going to be *okay*. Your life, your future, and your soul are at complete rest. It's a calming confidence you can carry, no matter what you're facing. *Although you may not be certain of what's to come, you can be certain of what's inside of yourself.*

I'm going to help bring out a force within you; a force so powerful that you can't even begin to imagine what you are able to create and everything you can become. My hope for you is that your inner voice becomes so strong that it's the only one you can *hear*. And you become so brave that your voice is the only one you *follow*. Let's not

simply accept only five per cent of our human potential ...
let's go for it all!

PART 4
Letting Go Of Suffering

I realize there's something incredibly honest about trees in winter, how they're experts at letting things go. - Jeffrey McDaniel

You and I naturally don't want to "let go" of anything. We have an ordinary habit of collecting and gathering; wanting to grasp and cling to things, ideas, possessions, etc. Essentially, it's because our human instinct is to survive, so we try to keep all that we can (like storing up for winter).

We become attached to things and sometimes it's impossible to let them go. Why would we want to let them go, anyway? For the simple reason that attachment produces suffering. It constrains us and keeps us closed to new possibilities. It's especially hard to let go when we have worked so hard to give these things form in the Universe. However, what if they were never ours to own? Is it likely that everything in our path is to simply be enjoyed as it comes? Perhaps all things in our material world are an illusion, and nothing is actually ours to keep?

Please trust me when I say it's as normal as breathing

to want to hang on to anything that may seem remotely comfortable and secure. After all, it is *you* that created it; it is *you* that birthed the idea, right? It's completely human of us to believe the fantasy that we have any sense of control – over anything. Still, to be able to learn the practice of letting go is a technique that could not only be life-changing but *life-saving*.

Hanging on creates suffering. Letting go is becoming free. People have fought wars for freedom. The ultimate liberty is just letting go. Don't start a war inside of yourself and create meaningless agony as a result of not letting go, especially when you can feel it's time. The only question now is: How do we know what and when to let go? This might challenge you. You might even get mad at me – I know. There is a tendency to pull something in even closer because someone's trying to take it from you. I promise you, I don't want it, I got my own stuff. What you keep so near to you, I don't desire in the slightest. By the end of this chapter, hopefully you won't either.

Let Go Of Your Anxiety

Millions of people in our world suffer from anxiety.

It is so sad and I can truly tell you I know what it's like. I feel like I was born anxious and it's been a fight ever since. In addition, our communication avenues seem endless these days; there is almost always someone or something that is competing for our attention. From our online digital worlds to our personal daily lives, it seems someone, from someplace, is longing for *something* of ours. And rightfully so, as we haven't created any boundaries around this issue and keep finding ourselves at the mercy of this awful addiction.

Anxiety is agonizing. It feels as if you are reaching for an item on a high shelf and no matter what you do you aren't getting any closer to it. Anxiety keeps you up at night because it doesn't allow you to feel safe enough to rest your head. You constantly feel as if you *have* to be doing something – at all times. It's the ever-present feeling that you have not done *enough*. So many young adults I talk to these days always feel like they could be doing *more*. Because technology never sleeps, apparently we have come to the conclusion that we shouldn't either. It sucks. It sucks all of your energy, your attention and focus. It forces you to make decisions based upon fear and worry, ultimately leading you down the path of destruction.

For years, anxiety was my home. It became normal to endure endless nights of on-my-face crying bouts because once again, I put too much on my schedule. The constant picking of my fingers until they bled and twirling my hair until it fell out became a horrible compulsion. I seriously believed if I *wasn't* overwhelmed or overthinking then something was wrong with me. It kept me safe because it was a familiar feeling and so the thought of letting it go scared me shitless. Until I realized that anxiety was taking over my life. I didn't have power over my anxiety; anxiety had power over *me*. So, it was time to put up a *For Sale* sign and move on. Actually, I had to put up a *Foreclosure, do not enter ever again,* sign.

We have to stop identifying with our anxiety and seeing it as a safe blanket with which we cover ourselves. Little do we realize we even use it as part of our personal introductions sometimes! "Hi, my name is Hailey, and I can't do x, y, and z, because I have anxiety." We protect it, as if it's doing any good for us. Although we may not say those exact words, it's an energy we keep unconsciously giving out without realizing it.

First we need to recognize the source of our anxiety. Why can't we rest? Why do we have this constant need to persist, to keep going and striving? Perhaps it's been your home, too, and it's the only way you know. But aren't you tired, tired of running and going around and around inside your hamster wheel that keeps you in the same place of distress and misery? Sometimes exhausted is the best thing to be because then it is easier to surrender. I've been there before so many times; burdened and so tired that I literally throw my hands in the air and exclaim, "Take this from me! I don't want the weight of this problem anymore!" Just so you know, it really helped, you should try it sometime.

When dealing with anxiety, think of the feeling as if it were a little child. Don't scold, punish, or beat it; instead, communicate *with* it. What would you say to that little child feeling anxious? Picture a meek and scared little girl or boy, six-years-old, standing right in front of you and full of nerves. What would you say to him or her? Can you nurture and encourage? Can you forgive? Let them know that it's all going to be okay and that this will pass. From this objective point of view you are able to console and recognize the intensity, without being swept away by its energy. By the way, if we have a tendency to scold the little child, chances are we treat ourselves the exact same way. It's the same for our pets; when I get irritated and short-tempered with my little puppy, chances are I've been treating myself the same way.

Inside each one of us is a little child who's experiencing this unease. It's your six-year-old Self that is experiencing this emotion. Don't try to suppress or eliminate the feeling; simply comfort and ask yourself, "What do I know for sure? What do I know to be true about what it is that I need right now?" And then, very delicately, you can say, "I want to give my heart fully, presently, right now, to this moment." You'll notice a shift in awareness and the emotion will eventually subside. Nothing (except Love) lasts forever; *this too shall pass.*

Think of silt that lies in a glass of water. When it is shaken and stirred up by emotions you tend to solve problems from your head. But when you go into stillness and return to the *now*, the dust settles and you are able to respond effectively and appropriately - from a centered place (your heart). Instead of being the one that is continually seeking answers or solutions, let them pop up within you and reveal themselves to you.

Whenever plagued by fear and anxiety, I take the advice of a wise friend and ask myself, "Is this really true? Is what I am feeling actually accurate?" In other words,

"Am I really going to die right now?" Anxiety begins in our thoughts and it usually goes something like this in our minds: "This shouldn't be. I am not enough. This is not enough. Why isn't this changing? I am not okay. I don't feel safe." Almost always these thoughts are not the truth about who you are or what is going on around you, and when you stop and ask yourself, "Now is this really true?," the pattern of your discomfort is interrupted.

The most effective and useful approach that works best for me is my breath. Anxiety is 100% in the body – it is physiological. If we can slow down our breathing, our anxiety will subside. Breath is our anchor and if we can remember this in any situation it can be our saving grace. Committing to peace is a moment-by-moment practice for our spirit.

Let's try this together right now. Breathe in slowly while silently counting in your head 1, 2, 3. Then breathe out slowly (as if you're cooling down hot coffee) counting 1, 2, 3 again. Drop your shoulders, relax your hands, and focus on your breaths. It also helps to be aware of your feet planted on the ground. Do this three times in a row. Notice how you feel. Observe the sensation in your body and mind. This is your tool to slowing down and making decisions from a clear space.

Anxiety is not our enemy; it's just energy. Whenever that feeling arises we must remember the little child within, and nurture it. We need to stop resisting it and *breathe into it*, until it passes. That's what it really means to let go of your anxiety. From a centered and unclouded space our creativity, freedom, and true joy emerges. By loving it, instead of fighting it, we gain so much more: Our peace of mind, imagination and inspiration.

Let Go Of Reacting

There is a difference between reacting and *responding*. The distinction is when you react, you say and act with whatever surfaces inside of you. When you *respond,* you think before you speak. Sounds simple, right? But it's almost never easy. As we get older we learn to tame our tongue a bit better (for fear of looking bad), and I'm not suggesting that we never speak our mind. In fact, I'm recommending the opposite. We want to share our hearts and what we feel is necessary to say; we just want to do it in a way that serves the greater good.

Things happen throughout our day that can easily

upset us. The weather isn't what we predicted or desired, we don't feel as respected as we should, people say something to us that undermines our authority, or just the mere fact that things don't go our way. All of these are examples that give us opportunities to react. They also give us a chance to respond – and to grow.

When faced with a situation that doesn't go according to your vision, the most enlightened way to handle it would be to let go of how you think things *should* be. The word "should" gets us into a lot of trouble because, the truth is, things will always be the way they are, not necessarily the way we want them to be. (More on that later.)

In order to achieve the best possible result, we have to let go of the way we want to react. We can only control how we *respond* to what happens in our lives. I believe we should always be free to share our minds – especially if it's something we absolutely believe in. Have you ever seen someone who was able to communicate in such a way that was incredibly persuasive and influential, yet wasn't manipulative or judgmental? These people rarely fail to accomplish their goals and achieve what they aspire.

The best thing to do is to take a breath, and then

pause and ask, "What is the best possible way to *respond* to this?" I promise the power of pausing could end up saving you much misery and shame. You won't have to look like a fool because you said something you wish you hadn't. You will apologize less, and be more conscious about how you treat others. Pick one person you completely trust, vent to them (release the emotions), and then let it go.

My grandfather always taught me growing up that it's okay to tell someone you need a day before you get back to them. He said you'll have a clearer head and mind and almost always have a better interaction and/or feeling about everything the next day. I call it the 24-hour rule. Wait 24 hours before responding to something you are not sure of. This enables you to act in a more mindful way. You can say, "Let me think on this, and I will get back to you tomorrow," (or any time frame that works well for you). Or, "I'd love to, unfortunately I don't have a definite answer right now – can I get back with you tomorrow?" Having one-line scripts will truly help you respond to what life throws at you because you'll honor yourself and be fully *prepared*.

Sometimes we get caught off guard so we say yes to avoid an awkward silence and then as soon as we walk away we think, "Crap, I didn't mean to say yes to that." Preparation breeds confidence for whatever may come up.

I know it's not easy in the moment, but the more you can catch yourself and develop a new habit of responding, the easier it gets. Besides, have you ever known a healthy response that stemmed from a reaction of anger? Let go of reacting and instead embrace a response.

Let Go Of Concepts And Ingrained Beliefs

Human beings have an incessant need to create meaning behind what happens to us. We find comfort in our thoughts and the things we tell ourselves to make us feel safe – and justified. So why would I recommend that we let go of them? Well, for the simple reason that they keep us from opening up. I've mentioned earlier in this book that the key to growing is remaining open to all things. In order to do that, occasionally, we must challenge our beliefs and ideas about life.

We ought to also forget about old beliefs and what we identify ourselves with. It could be hindering future opportunities that are looking to flock to us. Let me give you an example of what I mean.

At my previous job (I was a fundraiser,) my boss called me out of the blue and said, "I need you to come in the office and meet with a woman – her name is Sarah. She owns a non-profit and is struggling with asking people for donations, can you coach her?" I was happy to help. During our meeting I dedicated the first twenty minutes to simply listening to her. I wanted her to tell me everything about her company, what her barriers were, etc. She first introduced herself to me with her head down, body tight and said, "I'm just a retired math teacher trying to make a difference." I wanted to stop her right then and there – but I didn't. I listened to her heart and knew almost immediately what her setback was. It wasn't any of the many tribulations she described. It wasn't that her idea sucked (it was actually quite amazing); it wasn't that she hadn't been successful before (she had been in business for many years); it was one simple thing. She was operating on the *ingrained belief* that she was "just a retired math teacher." This effected how she communicated with everyone. We changed that by the time she left the office. A few weeks later she called me and said that things were transforming for her and she felt like a brand new person. That's because she was!

How many of you are moving through life with the notion that "All I am is_____"? Are you hanging on to someone you believe you should be, or how others want you to be? It's safe inside of your beliefs, I know. Inside of your concepts about who you are and what you're capable of it's nice and warm and stress-free. But is it really? Is it really serving you and the world?

I know deep down that each of you want to make an incredible difference in this world, or at least *someone's* world. However, we must let go of our embedded beliefs about ourselves. We are not our opinions; we are so much more. When it comes to becoming our highest Selves, particular views keep us trapped. If your belief about yourself produces an empowering emotion, then it serves a purpose; like the fact that you are powerful, perfectly designed and enough just the way you are. You can keep that one – that one *works*.

Let Go Of The Outcome

"Be patient, everything is coming together." I can't tell you how many times I heard this phrase and how each time it made me madder and madder. I was sick of people telling me everything was going to be fine, because I was truly afraid that it wouldn't be. I eventually realized that there was only one thing I needed to do: Let go of the outcome, and the rest would gently fall into place.

So often, we get in our own way. If we let things happen effortlessly, ultimately they work themselves out; but we get in the way by placing so much importance on "What happens IF?" I call this the "What IF danger trap." We say, "What happens IF this fails?," "What happens IF no one notices?," "What IF no one sees the importance of this, or even cares?," "Oh, what IF they reject me?!"

If you must ask "what IF," then please ask it this way: "What IF there is more coming than I could ever predict or desire?," "What IF the outcome surpasses my imagination?," "What IF I succeed and it all turns to gold?," "Even if it doesn't work out, what IF I was ok with it?," "What IF I start again – even if I don't get the result I'm anticipating?"

Maybe we are asking the wrong questions! All it takes is a simple shift in perspective to get the messages we so desperately need. This mindset move can make all the difference.

Can I just be straight with you? I know that what

you have created (or are in the process of creating), what you have finished, or what you are waiting for *will come*. It will come if it is a part of your destiny and if it's in your cards. And it might also not come; if it doesn't, then it's not what you needed. And always remember, you don't attract what you want, you attract *who you are*. Meaning, the most important question we could ever ask ourselves is, "Who am I being in this world? What type of person do I choose to be today?"

We want things to go our way. We have plans and some of us try to rearrange everything so that it will all go according to our specific plans. I've got news – it rarely ever goes the way you intended. As the saying goes, "We plan. God laughs." There are many bumps along the way and it gets ugly. My sweetheart said something so beautiful to me when I was caught in a worried phase of my life. I was in-between jobs, things weren't coming through, and my life was so messy. He said to me, "Hailey, did you know that nothing in nature grows in a straight line? Not one thing." I absolutely loved this. It gave my heart such peace. Our lives, our messy screwed-up lives, will never look perfect or predictable. We will have many turns, many setbacks, and lots and lots of thorns. You'll go down a path here, and a path there and eventually it will lead to your ultimate destiny. It'll be like this for the rest of your life. Perhaps our destiny is to become the highest version of truest Self. *Enjoy* it. Enjoy the mystery of the turns.

We must put forth the effort anyway. Build, craft, create, construct a masterpiece and then let go of the outcome. In fact, *anything* you put energy into – simply let go of what may come. Say out loud: "I've done this work, made this effort, created my truth, and now I surrender to what's to come."

It was Aristotle who said, *"Pleasure in the job puts perfection in the work."* We get so caught up in the end result that we cannot focus on the joy that comes with crafting the art. So might we throw out perfection and experience the sheer pleasure in the creation part of our beautiful work? In doing so, we attain inner peace.

Seek to be your best, most unperfected, and messy version of yourself, with pure intentions, and it'll be easier to forget about the outcome. Adopt a deep knowing that all which comes your way is unfolding in impeccable order, that all is well. *Because it is.*

Let Go Of What "Should Be"

I don't think many of us realize how often we say; "It shouldn't be this way." Adyashanti once said, "If you should have you would have;" meaning that any decision you made in the moments of your life was the one you were supposed to make. We may never understand the reasoning behind why we made a certain choice. This is where acceptance of "what is" comes into play. As my mama used to say growing up, "It is what it is, honey, and there ain't nothing you can do about it now."

Go for the ride. Instead of waiting, just purely say to yourself: *"Okay this is it for right now."* Memorize this line: *"This is it for right now."* Say it as many times as you may need. By doing so, you eliminate wanting to change the way things are. In fact, you might as well take the word "should" right out of your vocabulary (if that's possible for you).

Let Go Of Complaining

I tried an experiment while writing this book. For one day I decided to notice all of the times that I complained. I never thought I was a complainer. I thought that was everyone else's problem. Once I brought this to my awareness, however, I was shocked at how many times I actually criticized myself and what was happening around me. I was either too hot or too cold. That person gave me a bitchy look. I felt fat. My hair was a mess. The weather could have been brighter. You name it – it was the little things that I held onto. But it dramatically affected my attitude.

Try this same experiment yourself. How many times today do you complain about something? No matter how small, it still plays a part. Being unaware of what is going on inside of our minds, or the words that we speak, can be dangerous. As soon as you recognize your complaints they have no power over you anymore. Because now you have a choice whether or not you want to continue with that thought. When you become aware, you interrupt the pattern and can start fresh. Ahh, I can already smell the peace that comes with that. People will be attracted to you; they will sense the freedom that seeps from your bones and the joy you carry with you. Who wouldn't want that? The easiest way to shift your complaints into power is appreciation. Instead of focusing on what you have to complain about, focus on all that you have to be grateful for. I mean everything; your eyes to see, your ears to hear, your tongue to taste. Could you imagine having no taste buds?! The breath you breathe. It's so easy to take our miraculous lives for granted.

I remember a trip I took with my mother to North Carolina; the weather was so crappy. We left Michigan hoping to escape the dreary weather and ended up bringing it with us. We were sitting in our hotel room complaining of how we wished things were different. Because I was aware, I shifted and said, "Mom, how about just for five minutes we say everything we are grateful for?" She agreed, so we started naming everything we appreciated: our hotel room, the gas in our vehicle, our safety, our food, and for just being together. Soon we were rolling on the floor laughing (my mom's hilarious!), and we were so happy to be there. Our energy shifted immediately.

Yes, it's really this easy. Notice the words you use, the thoughts you think, and how you respond to the question, "How are you doing?" We have to remind ourselves that complaining only brings selfishness and more negativity in our lives. Let go of it and instead seek gratitude.

Let Go Of Addictions And Bad Habits

I am a recovering addict. The urge is still there, it comes all the time. Every day I have a choice whether or not to feed into it, and every day I choose to keep it at bay. You see, I was addicted to my cell phone; to technology.

Two moments stick out in my mind when I *knew* I needed to make a change. The first occurrence was pointed out to me by my long-time hairdresser as I was sitting in her chair. She's a kind-hearted, sweet lady with a lovely accent that could stop you in your tracks. But every time I sat in her chair I was glued to my phone. She'd ask me questions and I'd give half answers. She had to tell me numerous times to keep my head up because it was always face-down into my screen. I would rave to my friends about how good she was, but I rarely paid attention to her. One day she let me know, in the kindest way possible, that it was impolite to be on my phone while she was trying to talk with me. It doesn't seem like a big deal, but it hit me hard that day. I whispered, "I am so sorry. If I need to be on my phone, all I had to do was communicate that to you." But even after I went home I was still thinking about it. It was one of those small but insightful, significant, pivotal moments.

I started to think of all the times in my life when I had done this while people were trying to connect with me. It has become a norm in our culture to be on our phones, thus I hadn't even realized it was a problem. This discovery about myself led me to pay very close attention to my urges and how often I was attached to my phone.

The second occurrence was when I participated in a leadership-training program. We were instructed to ask our significant other or a family member if they thought we were a good listener. I always considered myself a great listener so I was pretty confident when asking my boyfriend what he thought. So very gently and considerately he confided, "About 70 per cent of the time I feel ignored." I instantly began to cry. The man I love told me he felt overlooked. Isn't it interesting how differently we can see ourselves through our eyes versus another? I knew something had to change.

It's unbelievable what can happen with a simple shift in awareness. What about you? What percentage of the time do you think you are really, whole-heartedly listening? How often are you truly present or only half-listening? Just ask – you might be shocked by the truth.

I bring the addiction of technology up because I believe it to be an epidemic in the younger generation today – maybe even beyond that. And believe it or not, the upcoming generation is called… are you ready for this? … *Digital Natives.* It is a wide-spreading addiction on the rise and the fact that it is an addiction is going unnoticed.

We need to let go of the control that technology has over our lives, and that begins with the realization that there is a problem. It's not necessarily a bad thing, we simply need boundaries. We need to know when it's time to put the phone down and pay attention. Once you become aware, the urge will still be there; someone will be speaking to you and you'll pretend to listen with your phone in your hand. Resist the constant technology itch and pretty soon it won't have control over you – you will have control over it.

Why is setting boundaries so important? For the simple reason that we cannot be completely fulfilled by, or connected to, a screen. It is a fascinating tool and incredible resource, but only through touch, and looking at someone deep within his or her eyes, can we experience the true Source.

Let Go Of Past Hurts

Oh, I can sincerely say I know this is a hard one for people. I still battle with this one from time to time. It was especially hard for me as a young teenager – pained by the past and not knowing how to move on. People know their own struggle stories – and they know them well. They know every detail of their pain; they relive memories countless times in their mind and cannot seem to shake the sadness.

Our loved ones, old relationships or guilt, and resentments we have built up toward ourselves can cause past hurts. Every wrongdoing or heartbreak we endure adds another strike to our board of pain. And every time it happens, we close up a little bit more. We get tighter and tighter.

Pain is inevitable in life; pain from people we love, from unrealized expectations, and the self-inflicted pain of regret and guilt. Forgive yourself, for you are doing the best you can. Love yourself, for you are the only one who truly can. Show your beautiful soul some compassion because we need you in this world; we need you to show up strong and gentle.

I have a friend who grew up without a father and it haunts her to this day. She has searched for security and her own worth in men who continue to let her down. If she were to just let go of the hurt she feels so deep inside, she would realize how open and beautiful she could become. It's not easy to let go of our past hurts – it could potentially be one of the hardest things we ever have to do. The key to remember is the word: PAST. It's in the past and that is where it should stay.

When we get hurt, especially from a loved one or family member, it's so easy to grip bitterness. Many people don't want to forgive because they think it lets the other person off the hook. "But they hurt me very badly. I'm pissed. I'm angry. I'm broken. I'm bruised. You're telling me that I'm just supposed to let it go?" Yes. With a lot of prayer, help from others, communication, or even therapy; yes, it is our job to let it go. Revenge and justice are not ours to dish out: that's God's job. Besides, bitterness is a slow poison and it's deadly. Do *yourself* a favor, and forgive.

I'm not proclaiming that this process will be easy; it most certainly will not. *But it's possible.* Cling to what is possible – not to what is easy.

Let Go Of Resentments

So often our resentments come from our past hurts. We have simple requests of people – and they let us down. Our simple requests are for others to love us (is that too much to ask?); for trust and respect (why is that so tough?). All we ask of people is to treat us kindly and with compassion – but they don't, again and again.

So guess what we do? We store in our minds all of their wrongdoings; all of the hurt feelings of being mistreated and eventually they bubble over into resentment. We hang on to them so firmly because we just can't believe how neglected and wronged we were and how angry we are. The anger seems so real; it feels so real. Although we believe that is serves us somehow, it doesn't. On the contrary, it destroys us. The resentment is actually gradually killing us. Letting go of the resentment doesn't help or hurt the other person, but it *heals* us.

No matter how hard we fight to change the way things are, or to change what has happened to us, we simply cannot. Hanging on to the cynicism within us doesn't help us grow to the next level. It keeps us stuck. Forgive yourself for holding on so tightly – you haven't known any differently. Begin by closing your eyes and placing your hand over your heart, then take a breath. Repeat slowly and softly to yourself: *I forgive you, I forgive you, I forgive you.* Then think of the person you are angry toward and say the same thing: *I forgive you, I forgive you, I forgive you.* Continue to feel your heartbeat and start to shift your mind to all you are grateful for.

Ultimately, the person we have to forgive is ourselves for hanging on so tightly. Our pain can be transformative. Run toward the pain, find what you must learn from it. Be changed by it. Ask, "What is the lesson here for me?" Your unlimited power, your peace and your *life* depend on it.

Let Go Of Recognition

He stood at the front of the store with a smile as big as the sun, waving to every single person that walked in the door. His job was to acknowledge everyone that entered, and he was the best damn "greeter" I've ever seen. Yet during the ten minutes I watched him, not one person noticed him.

This fueled anger inside of me. *Why was no one seeing this man? Why didn't they wave back? Why didn't they say "hi" and enjoy his presence?* I wanted to stand right up there with him and get in peoples' faces and make them see us, but instead I took a breath and practiced patience. I decided to turn my attention to the entrance to actually see who was walking inside.

First, I noticed a businessman that kept glancing at his watch and looked like he was in a hurry (perhaps he was in charge of donuts for a meeting he was running late for). Then I observed a mother who had a cart full of kicking and screaming kids. She was rummaging through her purse, maybe searching for a grocery list while attempting to keep all the little arms and legs inside the moving vehicle. She may have been a single mom who had no option but to take the kids with her (hardest job in the world – I watched my mom raise five of us).

I then witnessed a couple who looked to be so in love that even if the greeter was standing there with a sign that had their names in bright red – they still wouldn't have seen him. They encapsulated my attention all together– I just love, love. And I love seeing others that love each other so much they live in worlds of their own. Smiling into one another's eyes – how could they possibly have noticed him?

Soon after I stopped watching, I turned my attention back to the greeter. He was an unbelievable man. No matter who walked through the door, no matter what baggage they were bringing with them or what they looked like, this man treated each of them the same. He was so awake to life, so kind and conscious to the real meaning of love (little did he know). His arms were open and ready to pour into anyone, no matter who they were; *even though he was being ignored.*

On days when I find myself judging others, and when my patience is awfully low, I think of this man. I remember that he gave without any expectation of return. I remember how his smile wasn't dependent upon others smiling back. I think of how his joy radiated from the inside out. That "greeter" is perhaps the embodiment of truth. This will happen to you, too. You will show love and get nothing in return. You will smile and not get one back – you might even be completely ignored. You'll open your arms and people will walk by.

At the end of the day it's not about how others receive you – it is about one thing and one thing only:

Choosing to shine anyway. If you can consistently remember who you really are: A creation of God and a walking miracle – you'll never need recognition again.

Let Go Of Your Desires And Dreams

Let's take a moment right now ... I'd like you to think of your dreams. What do you greatly desire? What do you long for? What wishes keep you up at night? If it helps to make a list of each individual dream and desire, do so. Try free-flowing your thoughts on paper; grab and sheet and a pen and for 10 minutes write down all of what you desire in your life. Do you desire a form of relief in a particular situation? Do you desperately want something so much that it's starting to become an obsession? Once you have answered these questions then let's continue.

Take a look at what you have before you. I so deeply believe that each dream and desire has been divinely and strategically placed within you. They've been woven and ingrained into your heart by design so therefore you need not to worry – you are not alone in this venture. Basically, it's not your fault you aspire what you do. Technically speaking, you didn't choose them, you were born with them. Why do you think our dreams differ from others?

Consider that everything you want has its own perfect timing when it's supposed to emerge in your life. It's not our job to control what happens or dictate the steps along the way – it is only our duty to carry forth and hold the dream.

This might be the hardest thing to learn to do in your lifetime – surrender your dreams and desires. There's an old Buddhist saying, "The root of all suffering is desire." How can we possibly not hold tight to our imaginings? The simple truth I realized that helped me understand why I should let it go is this: There could be *so much more* for my life that my human mind cannot conceive on its own. Living this life is a partnership with creation – we are co-creating with God. The human mind can only envision a piece of what is to come. By surrendering your dreams and desires, you open up a field of all possibilities – leaving everything undone and unseen. Essentially, you allow the world to work in your favor and reveal all the miracles it wants to shower upon you. Nothing is impossible when you give up control of what's to come. Throughout my life, my heart has leaned on Matthew 19:26: "With God, all things are possible." *How magical is that?*

Goals and dreams are still very important to hold close to you. Take this book for example; if I hadn't set goals along the way I probably wouldn't have finished – or it would have taken me many more years.

Cherish your dreams and desires and make sure to check in on them during different seasons of your life – you may want to alter them along the way. Ultimately, we want to stay detached and not worry so much about the when and how, but focus on the long-term vision. If it helps, you can say these words: "I can now let all of this go because what is to come will come and what I am *meant* to do will happen. So whatever comes my way today I know is the right thing at this time." Put them in a special place in your heart, but then let go so you can sit back and witness the mystery of all that can be.

Let Go Of The Need To Know What Your Future Entails

There is one similarity in all of our lives: The time we are given. We all have the same 24-hour day, one day at a time. Young and old alike are incessantly planning for the future; picking a career, raising a family, planning for retirement … it's never ending. We become bonded to our future and it can come with a tremendous amount of pressure. How are we supposed to know exactly how it will all turn out? What if life knows exactly what it's doing and all you need to do is let go of the worry about what is to come? Marianne Williamson, international author and lecturer once said, "Worrying is a way of praying for the worst outcome." How *awesome* is this?

I'd like to offer a new perspective that has changed how I view my future: What if we see purpose in each *step* along the way? So instead of achieving one sole purpose in your entire lifetime, what if there are multiple milestones along your journey? I heard this quote the other day, "Life isn't about the journey or the destination – it's about the checkpoints." I just *love* that! There is meaning in each checkpoint you reach – marvel in *those* moments.

Let me ask you this, what are you doing right now? In this very moment, what are you doing? Are you eating while you read?, sitting?, lying down? Your purpose for this moment, and this moment only, is reading this book. That's all there is right now. Someone could come knocking at your door any second and change the next couple of hours, or the entire course of your day. You might have little ones about to awake from a nap, or a little puppy that needs attending to. Or, if you're outside, a torrential rainstorm could occur in just a few minutes. You just never know.

The truth is that each phase and period of your time here leads you to the next chapter, and the next chapter, and that's all you need to know. Essentially, that's all we *get* to know. I know, it sucks; because human beings have a persistent need for assurance in their lives. No matter how much we demand to know what our life will look like five, ten, or twenty years from now, we never will. So make plans, create a vision, and then let go of it all and live.

Let Go Of Needing To Be Right

Do you like to be right? Do you just love that sweet satisfaction of getting in the last word and being spot-on? I bet every person has said yes to this question. To some, being right is an addiction. That satisfied feeling you get right after saying something that shuts the other person right up doesn't last very long … 30 seconds?, a minute? Pretty soon you need to be "right" again. It's a never ending cycle that leaves us unfulfilled and tears up relationships.

Needing to be right creates a strong division between two people. You can only see one way – and it *must* be the one true way. Clinging to our judgments generates separation and more often than not we are operating inside of our Egos (our small, worldly Selves). If we aim for inner peace, we have to get comfortable seeing another point of view, or at least respecting it.

At the Source, there is no "other side," it is merely an illusion. We can never attain peace if we are stuck on needing to be right. Instead, try for kindness; try to validate the other being that is standing in front of you by saying, "Wow. I've never thought of it like that. Tell me, how did you come to that conclusion?" Do you know how powerful those words are? You will be exponentially surprised at what power you can create by doing this instead of feeding the addiction to be right.

Eventually, we need to ask one simple question: "Is being *right* worth giving up my long-term happiness and the existence of this relationship?"

Let Go Of The Need To Rush (Hurry – Read This One!)

I know it appears we don't have time for much anymore - "there isn't enough time in a day" as the expression goes. Nevertheless, some of us do try to cram it all into one day. We are like little bees flying from flower to flower, rushing around trying to finish; to accomplish; to get things done.

There is nothing wrong with maximizing your time; it is one of the most precious things we have on this earth. However, let's visualize the rushed person; they are not hard to spot in this day and age. I used to work with a woman who appeared to be a tornado ripping through the building every time she entered. She wasn't just in a hurry; she was moving so fast from one thing to the next that she never fully experienced any lasting joy. In attempting to talk with her you realized that her body was there, but her mind and presence were not. Have you ever met someone like this?

I think it's important to recognize that great things still take time. In our culture today, we are so used to everything happening with a push of a button. With a tap of a finger, something happens. And bam, just like that, we get a result. This creates a sense of instantaneous reaction. Life doesn't always work that way, though. Things take time and we still need to cultivate a sense of patience and ability to wait or we will *never* find peace. Consider that waiting may be the most spiritual thing we could ever do. It is during the waiting period that our souls germinate and our seeds of actions start to sprout. Give the Universe time to catch up to you. Waiting is not doing nothing. Waiting is doing everything.

Although we want to get the most out of each day, we cannot be slaves to time. Some projects will take days or weeks, others will take years; but it's better to do something right than to allow the time it takes to control you. A sense of urgency comes from within. We are the ones who create it. Therefore, we are the ones who can choose peace instead. We can *choose* to slow down. We *must* choose to slow down, especially in the process of our creative ventures. We can't rush or force our agenda on inspiration because we are on a time schedule... we have to flow *with* it. On the other hand, in the past I have used my innate sense of urgency as a way to fuel my ambition. *That is not wrong to do.* We simply need to be conscious of when it's the right time to hurry and when we should slow down. You control the speeds.

Next time you find yourself in a situation that makes you feel tense or frustrated or hurried, try to stop yourself in action. Take a breath, or many breaths, and slow down. My dear childhood friend suggested that I practice walking backward because I moved so fast. It truly helped me slow down. Of course I don't have the best balance, but the concept has helped me move slower in life and enjoy every bit of the experience. Another thing I do is chant, "One thing at a time, one thing at a time, one thing at a time…" all day long. It works like magic and I am immediately reminded to be conscious of the activity and not just moving on autopilot. I'm also reminded to *be slow to anger* and *slow to speak, quick to listen.* It never fails me when I take a step back and move consciously though my life, fulfillment follows.

The Body Tells Us When It's Time To Let Go

We all have internal compasses, essentially those are our inner voices. We have inner dialog that is always communicating with us. That's why it's so important to develop such a strong internal world, above all else. Some call it the Holy Spirit, Intuition, or The Small Still Voice; it doesn't really matter; all that's important is being aware of its presence. Our body gives us the first signal that it's time to let go.

The key is to watch for any signs of contracting in the body and then releasing it; make your hand into a tight fist and then turn it upward and open it softly in a giving way…this is the simplest way to contrast between contracting (holding on) and letting go. It helps to picture what you want clenched tight between your fingers, and then opening the palm and mentally releasing it. Whenever you can associate letting go (of anything) with a physical movement, it truly helps.

Feeling frustrated, annoyed, stuck, fearful, anxious, stressed or overwhelmed are sure signs that there is something inside of us that we need to let go of. Pay close attention to what is going on inside of you; set reminders for yourself to check on how you're feeling. Are you tight, closed off, shy or nervous? Or are you peaceful, calm, hopeful and expectant? Don't fight what you feel, relax into it; and you'll notice a shift in your body. Try not to ignore the signs.

Let Go Of Jealousy

Jealousy and envy are very dangerous feelings – if acted upon. I know the feeling of jealousy and I know it well. I also know (thank God) that in those moments I *have* to do something about it otherwise it will eat me alive.

Here is what it does to us: It instantly creates an awful feeling of unworthiness, making us feel that because somebody else has something we desire – we cannot have it either. It also generates a deep-rooted feeling of scarcity, providing us the illusion that there is not enough. It can even make us sick. It stirs up an emotion of loneliness that everyone else is getting something and we are being left out. It generates fear, ferocious anxiety, and brokenness; we must learn how to handle this acquaintance that is not welcomed at this party.

First, you've got to *get it out*. Emotions are released in several ways and it's up to you to take control of them or they will go haywire. You've got to tell someone (just *one* person) you completely trust about your feelings of inadequacy and jealousy. Simply verbalizing your feelings can release the hold they have on you. Often times you are able to see how ridiculous your inner fears are. If you don't have that one person, or aren't able to connect with them at the time, *write it down.* That is also a healthy form of relief. You can start at the top of your paper, "Dear Jealousy…" and talk through how you are feeling, perhaps why you might be feeling that way and then simply sit with it. Jealousy is a form of pain and it comes rushing in and so we try to get rid of it immediately because we hate the way it makes us feel. However, I would encourage you to be still with it and do your best not to shame yourself for it.

Secondly, I want you to consider that your feeling of envy is trying to teach you something. Perhaps it's a gift rather than a difficulty. It might be shining a bright light on what you know in your heart you can accomplish. Ask yourself, "Why am I feeling jealousy toward this person, idea, business, or possession?" Really search and listen for the answer; it might be an eye-opening exercise and awakening for you, and it just might be the thing to get you up and running again.

Listen to me; you are *worthy*, you are *included* and you are *enough*. It will be your time soon. My therapist looked me deeply in the eyes one day and said, "Hailey, rejoice for the people who have what you want right now, because one day it will be your turn, too. And remember that we are all connected, so when one shines – we all shine." Boy, did those words pierce through me like ice cold water striking my skin. Please take these words in as you read them, and remember that there is room for you at the table – there **is** room for you, too.

We Can Let Go By Remembering

Underneath each aspect of your life – working, thinking, pursuing and your intellect – is the need to surrender and *feel*. Beneath all of our daily habits and routines is a part of us that wants to feel deeply rooted and united to the vulnerability of our hearts. There are moments and times in our lives when we are gently swayed to remember: To remember the essence of what is begging to be shared and felt; to experience the emotion of softness and to feel the irresistible feeling of connectedness.

Think about the times you've allowed yourself to go "there;" to the place that may not be socially acceptable or professional that wants to play, explore and connect deeply with another. Can you picture this?

Very often, during a conversation or a memory, you can remember what it is truly like to fully embrace the beauty of the moment. Perhaps you can remember when you lost someone dear to you and closed yourself off to sadness or grief; or a time when you were in the midst of expressing love and appreciation to another; or the time you held your first child. This idea of remembering brings us back to the core of what we long to experience and about how precious our lives are. To remember is to experience life fully.

On the topic of remembering, don't forget to be easy on your sweet Self. Without even recognizing it we criticize ourselves for the littlest things. You are *learning* – every day, so relax into the process of absorbing and transforming. And if you can soften and stay open; slowly and surely you will come to be at peace with the person you are and the person you're becoming.

When was the last time you let yourself go? When you allowed yourself to play, dance and be free from all your duties and "responsibilities?" To play, laugh, and to remember brings us back to the Source of who we really are and from where we originated.

Let Go of Your Suffering

Becoming aware of what causes chaos in our lives is the first step to releasing the hold it has over us. We have to recognize when the discomfort surfaces – what's going on inside our bodies? Can we feel the anger start to rise, palms getting sweaty, or our insides tighten? Next time something happens that gets your blood boiling, practice witnessing what's going on. It's sometimes comical what makes us tick, isn't it?!

I can truly empathize that letting go of what makes you suffer is an incredibly difficult task. It's one thing to read it, and another to do your best to practice it moment-by-moment. Even now, I'm sitting in my sanctuary (aka: the library) writing this book and I have subtle feelings of discomfort. I have to let that go too. It may seem easier to simply keep doing what you've been doing, but I can be the first to tell you it's worth it to at least try.

Make no mistake, there is no quick fix for our pain. There is not an "end goal" or a "light at the end of the tunnel." We're walking this tunnel our entire lives, and it's what we do *during* the passing time that determines our freedom. What's the benefit of letting go? It's simple: Inner freedom. Freedom from having to defend our actions. Freedom from explaining every detail *why* we make the choices we do. And freedom of being able to go anywhere at anytime with a confident knowing of how valuable we are, and not giving a damn what another person says or does about it. Go freedom!

Put Your Stamp On This World!

While on a road trip I came across a billboard which read, in big, bold, bright letters, "PUT YOUR STAMP ON THIS WORLD." Silently, I thought, "Yes, Yes, YES!" I was motivated by these words. "What's my stamp?," I wondered. I had heard this expression before, but for some reason this time was different. You can hear something over and over again and it doesn't resonate, but suddenly you'll hear it from some other place and it all clicks. There's a saying, "When the student is ready, the teacher will appear." It doesn't matter how many times you have heard something; unless you are in a place to receive, you won't. Getting into a place to receive is simply being open and authentically listening. In other words, being in awe of what is being shared with you. This was one of those receiving moments for me.

It started me thinking a bit deeper; all of us just truly want to know we made a difference and that our lives mattered. Therefore, I say to you, put your stamp on this world! Let people know that you are here, and you're not leaving until you've done what you came to do. No matter what you do in this world – big or small – make it count; do it with the greatest *love*, enthusiasm, and joy you possibly can. Do it with a pure heart and wholesome intentions, not for power or an ingrained belief.

Throughout your life there will be ups and downs and in-betweens. Our job is to let what goes, go; to witness what comes and to welcome it, and then pay attention to what remains. The internal struggle of conflict no longer has a stronghold on our heart if we choose to let go. Things will disturb your inner peace on a daily basis, witness the emotion and allow it to pass. We can live beautiful lives, we were not made to suffer. But we are so familiar with our suffering that it scares us to let it go. The only freedom we will ever find is right past our self-inflicted suffering.

In fact, sometimes our strong will to let go interferes with the action of letting go; therefore, let go of letting go, release the worry and pressures of having to be perfect. Lift the burden off your heart to "do it right" and simply honor your own path towards growth.

Past hurts don't serve our future. Resentments don't make us feel more loved. Judgments don't make us more connected. Jealousy doesn't get us what we want. The addictive need to be right destroys relationships. Trying to control the outcome does not give us peace. Receiving recognition doesn't improve self-worth – that's our job. And holding on so strongly to things that aren't ours to keep is a complete waste of our miraculous lives.

"Having nothing to attack, nothing to defend, nothing to conceal, and no interests to guard, they are at peace."
– James Allen

PART 5
Embrace Silence And Your Inner Voice

"Meditation is not about creating a stillness or quiet in the mind, but touching into the stillness that is already there." – Adyashanti

Imagine yourself as a person who is always producing the highest good, for yourself and the planet. Everywhere you go, you carry a calming confidence and are able to have an immediate and effective influence on those around you. When people see you, they think to themselves, "What is it about them that I find myself wanting?" This potential lies within you; this is true power.

Imagine a well full of silence that you can go to and use to replenish your infinite soul. This well is deep, vast, and ever expanding. There is no concern of this well running dry – it's continually filled and is eternally offering. Human beings have an innate desire for silence; it is what allows us to tap into an infinite resource of joy, inspiration and peace.

What Is Silence?

Silence can also be described as stillness. Silence is getting to the place where you reconnect with yourself. Whether you're experiencing a great sense of pleasure and you want to fully embrace the moment, or feeling stressed out and burdened, moments of silence can help us feel alive and awakened. I was initially attracted to this concept because of my anxiety. Even now, it comes in waves, but I have this to lean on when I feel as if I am sinking in sand.

I needed something that could forever impact my life. I needed a real solution, not just a Band-Aid. Often times, it takes hopelessness and feeling immobilized before we can see that we must do something *else*. All we know is that whatever we are doing is not working. There may be something inside of you that aches for resolution; you're longing not to be pulled in every direction. Perhaps you're growing weary and need rest; or possibly everything about your life is fulfilling, yet you still have the need for more growth.

It's often that people actively avoid silence, some cannot even stand it. As soon as there is a moment of quietness we try to fill the void up in some way. Instead, we check our watch, instinctively reach for our phone, tap our foot, call a friend, or start another project. One woman confided to me that times of stillness makes her crazy. She literally panics and can't even sit on her couch for five minutes before she's ready to get up and get going again.

There is a reluctance we have towards silence. It's possible that we are afraid of what may surface. Being still forces us to be with ourselves and only us. It's an intimate time and very vulnerable. We don't want to be alone with our thoughts because of what may come up. What would reveal itself to you that you don't want to see?

Some people also mistake alone time as loneliness. There is a big difference. Overcoming the feeling of loneliness is an inside job. It's actually quite ironic because in order to feel *whole*, sometimes we have to go inward *alone*.

Although, there is no denying the incredible benefits you receive when you talk out what's going on inside with a close-trusted friend or a respectable professional. Having the courage to speak about your inner journey is transformational. There are plenty of conversations I've had and right in mid-sentence I'll receive the breakthrough I was searching for. If you struggle with silence, continue to stay open and ease into the discomfort.

There are some outward signs which indicate that we need to unite to our true nature again. Have you experienced any of these signs?

- Feeling frustrated for absolutely no reason.
- Becoming irritable or impatient with yourself and others.
- Finding alternatives to deal with stress (overeating or indulging in unhealthy activities).
- Criticizing yourself; subconsciously punishing yourself for doing or not doing something when you should be taking care of yourself in a way that nourishes you.
- Making unnecessary judgments about people.
- Feeling a desire to love more and express it more freely.

Something beautiful happens when we are awakened to a new possibility and perspective; when we realize that we don't want to suffer anymore and understand that we are deserving of true happiness. What if you *allowed* yourself to feel complete? How would your life change if you knew you were valuable and worthy to be truly happy?

We need to start making ourselves a priority and see how sincerely vital silence is for our health and well-being. Silence can be achieved in moments. When you're at a red light and your car is at a standstill, there's a moment for silence and a calming breath instead of grabbing quickly for your phone. When you catch yourself getting caught up in the emotion of a situation, that's a perfect time to take a deep breath and tune into yourself or silently pray. Experiencing a tremendous amount of joy and excitement is also worthy of silence – close your eyes and experience the magnitude of the moment.

Silence and Meditation Coincide

I'd like to share with you a basic tool that has changed my life: The art of meditation. To experience silence for a period of time is one of the most crucial habits I have adopted in my life. Quite frankly, it's been one of the most important instruments on this path of discovering who I am. It absolutely grounds me in peace and makes me feel weightless. I frequently call it, "My experience with God. My God time." His presence seems to be all over me as soon as I become still. I sit in my same red chair every time I "Go to meet with God." I tell you, some days I melt right into my chair and start sobbing because it feels much like I'm coming *home.*

I was born an anxious and action-oriented person (as you already know). For years I had heard/read about meditation, and yet never fully committed myself to it. I've never been one to sit still for a period of time, bouncing from one project to another, and from job to job. But for quite awhile now, I've taken the time to really make it a central part of my life.

Focusing on silence is honoring that part within you that needs alone time. It's being with yourself to see what's going on in there; what your body needs. Even if you are a busy mother/father, or working multiple jobs with excessive responsibilities, taking a step away for a moment, and a deep breath, can save your sanity.

My meditation practice has certainly evolved over time and yours will, too, so be patient. I will tell you this, I've come to a point where I can recognize that something is off with my body and/or emotions if I don't "go to my red chair."

Before I get too heavily into this topic, I'd like to tell you about the wise woman who's imparted this beautiful gift to me – my meditation teacher and one of the most wonderful souls I've ever known. She has been a teacher of meditation throughout the world for over forty years. While favoring the simple purity of the practice of Transcendental Meditation and the teachings of Maharishi Mahesh Yogi, she has also studied with other great teachers including; Muktananda, the Dalai Lama, and many teachers of both Tibetan and Zen Buddhism. She has done intensive retreats with Pir Vilayat and Adyashanti, completed Maharishi's Teacher Training and Siddhis courses, studied the teachings of Yogananda and was initiated into Kriya Yoga by Swami Prajnanananda. She has also received teachings in Ayurvedic medicine and primordial sound from Deepak Chopra.

With great gratitude and appreciation for all of these teachings she has grown to appreciate how, at their very depth, they all basically agree and can be verified by experience. But she feels that intellectual understanding is not as important as keeping it simple and just easily putting the awareness on the underlying silence.

She has a way about her that is completely non-threatening. Anyone who spends time with her senses the peace that radiates from her being. We have grown to be close friends and she has helped me to appreciate and confirm what I have experienced from meditation. I am excited to share with you some of her great wisdom that has so enriched my life.

For me, practicing silence and meditation takes me back to pure awareness where I am simply *being*. As a natural doer and constant mover in my life, this is essential. Beyond all the busyness and noise in life, meditation has been the anchor back to my authentic self. My teacher describes meditation using the analogy of an ocean: When you begin to quiet yourself, the waves of thought and activity are still present; tossing and tumultuous on the surface of the ocean. But as you sit still longer and longer, you begin to naturally gravitate deeper and deeper toward the bottom of the ocean where there is simply stillness and quiet. That space is the Source from which all creation emerges. It's important to recognize that meditation should be simple and effortless. Each time you begin to meditate, say to yourself, "Here goes nothing," and treat every experience as if it were your first time, like an innocent child that knows nothing about it. This will help you let go of any opinions of how your practice "should" go or if you're doing it "right" or "wrong."

No Particular Belief Or Lifestyle Required For Meditation

What if we experienced laughter more often? What if we played more? Had more joy in our lives? What could happen to your life if you knew how to change the energy of a moment? Through meditation I have increased my ability to live light and not carry around so much dead weight of frustration, guilt, and shame.

As you continue your practice of meditation, it's important to remember that you can return to this tool at any point in life. This life-changing skill is for everyone and anyone. You don't have to be a monk; you don't have to look or even act a certain way. Some of the best leaders of the world have incorporated this into their lives. There are no requirements – anyone can practice the art of meditation; it doesn't require any particular belief or lifestyle.

The more patience you have with your practice, and especially yourself, the sooner you'll begin to experience the direct benefits mediation has to offer. Sometimes I never want to leave this particular space, it feels *that* good.

With that being said, the more you experience the space of silence, the more you begin to take it into your daily actions and live with peace while encountering any situation.

The True Benefits Of Meditation

Research has shown improved mental abilities very soon after beginning the practice of meditation. We see these increases in our broader understanding, development of intelligence and creativity, enhanced ability to focus, better memory, organization of brain functioning, improved mind/body coordination and greater coherency in brain wave performance. As you know, I've struggled all my life with anxiety and medication did not fix it for me, it made me feel worse, actually. And I'm not saying that you should stop taking your medication (everyone is different); however in my experience meditation has been the most sustaining preventative.

Meditation has also been found to be a key to good health. All disease and sickness are stress related in some way, whether directly or indirectly. Meditation produces physiological effects in the body which are the exact opposite of those produced by stress. Over time, the state achieved during meditation remains within us as we go about our day: The nervous system becomes more flexible and no longer reacts to situations in the same stressful way; and we are able to see our circumstances from a new perspective which will allow new opportunities to flourish. Are you excited yet?

With the expansion of one's full mental potential, the view of the world changes so that things which once might have seemed stress-producing are now seen in terms of the big picture and do not pose the same threat. Not only does this greatly enhance the enjoyment of life, it also has a huge impact on our health and relationships.

The ultimate benefit, of course, comes from the realization of the true Self and the unlimited potential within. The awareness finally comes to rest in one's true essence instead of being caught up in all the little individual aspects of the personality that have been accumulating since birth. With the realization of our interconnectedness with everything comes an opening of the heart that is indescribable.

There are countless ways to meditate. I can only share with you what I've been taught and the techniques that work for me. Please take what resonates with you and set aside what doesn't. You may gather little pieces from this book and also from other fantastic resources on meditation that are available.

Mindfulness

Do you know what your blinker sounds like while driving your car? Can you feel your foot press against the gas pedal? Can you hear the sound the engine makes when it speeds up, or stops? Are you aware of your surroundings? Can you truly value what it is to simply touch something? Can you look at your hands with wonder and think, "There's so much I can do with these ... my hands are meant to create; my mouth is meant to speak."

I invite you to not only be mindful of the things that occur every day, but to be in awe of them. Look at things with wonder and excitement and joy and color. There is true power in recognizing that the life we get to live is so wonderful. Miracles happen every day and Love is present in even the smallest things. Your purpose is meant to be discovered in each moment, not just one giant moment in a lifetime. Meditation helps you to become mindful and experience the joy in any activity, no matter how minimal.

Here's How To Begin

The first step is to prepare prior to each meditation practice. Begin with a mindset of "Here goes nothing." Again, create an open mind as if it's the first time – every time. This will help you avoid judging what is going on inside of you. If possible, eliminate any likely distractions. Also, it's best not to eat a heavy meal beforehand. And most importantly, *seize the moment.* Even if it isn't feasible to remove all of the distractions, it's still best to meditate. It's always better to do it under any circumstance than to wait until everything is perfect.

Next, sit comfortably, either crossed-legged or in a chair where your back can be straight and your head is free to move. Gently close your eyes. Let your body be loose, with your arms so relaxed that if someone picked them up they'd be floppy. *Let the face beneath your skin and your eyes go soft and tender.*

Put your attention on your breath. Let it be at its natural depth and rate. Breathe relaxed so that your abdomen rises as you inhale. Notice the silence that is already present. If the mind seems busy, you might want to introduce a mantra – *So Hum* is a good, universal one to use. Sometimes, I simply meditate on the word *Jesus*; whatever is comfortable for you. The most important thing about a mantra is to think it gently and effortlessly. Don't concentrate on it or try hard to think it clearly. Let it change and disappear as it wishes. Just easily come back to it when your attention has started to focus on thoughts again. In the beginning, it might be helpful to attach *So Hum* to your breath; thinking *So* as you breathe in and *Hum* as you breathe out. However, remember your purpose in meditation is to experience the underlying silence that's always there, so in the end you want to let go of everything – including the mantra. You want to keep your body still as much as possible, but if something is bothering you - a cough, an itch, your leg falls asleep - it's best to rearrange so that you are comfortable.

I've been asked the question, "How do I come out of meditation?" The answer is simple – slowly and quietly. If you're using a timer it's best to have something with a soft tone, an alarm that isn't too jarring.

Start out meditating for fifteen to twenty minutes. Twenty minutes twice a day is said to be the ideal by many teachers, but trust your instincts and find what fits best in your life that you can do consistently. It's more important to develop the habit than to focus on concrete rules. During each practice, even if you're feeling restless, stay with it (no matter how hard it may be to sit still); something transformative is happening. Maharishi was a great teacher of Transcendental Meditation. He said if you're feeling restless during meditation, bear it patiently; something good is happening. Meditation will eternally be a cycle of inward and outward shifts of experiences.

The continuous purpose of stillness and quiet is simply embracing it – even though we experience countless distractions. Our power constantly materializes from the soundless. Learn to love the calmness that radiates from your soul.

Once you've experimented, you may want to use guided meditations, music, or simply remain on your own. A good "starter course" is to start with Oprah and Deepak Chopra's 21-Day Meditation Challenge. Deepak has studied primordial sounds and how the effect of different sounds changes our nervous systems. He and Oprah have teamed up together to create many powerful meditation challenges.

Over time, however, you will want to experience some solitude meditations where it is only you and pure silence. This is a meaningful process, and one that never stops evolving. As you grow in your practice you will start to know what is best for you.

An important fact to be aware of: The art of meditation is a very *patient* and *slow* process. If you want a quick fix, this is not it.

When first learning to meditate I picked up an amazing book entitled *Meditation*, by Eknath Easwaran – a spiritual teacher who has authored over a dozen books on ways to lead a meaningful life. In it he writes:

> "This is why I recommend do not fight distractions in meditation. If you do, you give them your attention, your vital energy, and they swell up with it and are harder than ever to dislodge."

He speaks a lot about watching what we give our attention to. When first starting out in meditation, we have a large amount of racing thoughts and it can be hard to manage them. Try to sit with your thoughts, ignore them, and don't be bothered by them because what you focus on multiplies. Favor the underlying silence that is always there. Shift your attention back to that silence every time your thoughts begin to race.

This is important: Studies have shown that there are measurable physiological health benefits from just sitting still even though you are experiencing a bombardment of thoughts … how cool is that? Thus, no meditation practice is ever wasted time or energy.

The more you sit quietly and embrace the silence and quiet moments of your life, the more you'll begin to relish and enjoy every aspect of your life … and see miracles in all you do. Being in meditation groups is also a powerful experience that I would strongly recommend. Where two or more are gathered, the effects are magnified and you are more strongly connected to the oneness with the Source. The presence of God there can seem to be quite tangible.

To put it simply, mediation is a personal practice. And yes, it is a practice. It's a journey of continuing to grow ourselves to the highest level. My teacher describes it as "A direct experience with our Source and your true essence. It also provides a way of contributing to the *world*." For me, it takes me back to the center and root of who I really am, grounds me in my truth, and calms my spirit in a very demanding world. It allows positivity to radiate more easily in my life. What are your beliefs about meditation? Can you afford *not* to incorporate this tool in your life?

We Are the Actor, Director, *And* The Audience

My teacher gave me this wonderful analogy that I am pleased to pass along to you; it has helped me so much. There are three parts of ourselves that make up who we are: The actor, the director, and the audience. What does this mean and how do they apply to our lives?

Actor: When dealing with our small selves there is some part of us that are actors, acting in this drama of life. We come here, accepting our parts like pieces of a giant puzzle. She suggests that we should live it dynamically and wonderfully, participating as powerfully and dramatically as we can, without getting so caught up that we lose sight of our true selves. You know, "Live life to its fullest." This is the part that is a temporary manifestation and yet we can be dedicated to making it the best play ever.

Director: The director side of us is our intellect, our mind, everything that we have learned and programmed into our brains. The intellect clarifies and distinguishes for the actor and is the part that guides actions. This is the part that has a plan and executes it to the best of our ability. It also helps direct the actor to make wise choices.

Audience: This is the highest part of ourselves. This is the part that is the pure awareness that observes all aspects of life. When in the present moment, this is the part that is pure consciousness. This is our ability to see everything in terms of the bigger picture and the vision of all possibilities. (In other words, seeing the present moment in terms of everything that ever was, is, and ever will be.) The audience is the part of us that truly experiences enjoyment; the place from which you want your creativity and inspiration to originate. From this standpoint, wherever we go, we can experience our interconnectedness with everybody. We are able to be the observer and this is the home to come back to; the home from which we act and direct our lives, and where we feel the most welcomed, whole and complete. We want to try to live here the most. As we are being the actor and the director, we are living from the place of the audience and are not lost in the drama therefore not letting it take over our lives.

Another way to describe this is to think about when you are watching a movie. From your perspective you can fully understand all three concepts. The actor is the person you are watching on the screen; the one that is fully engaged in the entertaining and exciting part of the drama of life. The director brings out the best in the actor and tells him or her which way to go. And you, as an audience member, are fully aware and can appreciate all of it. From this angle you can see the whole, and you can see it clearly.

It's wonderful to have these three distinctions because we were meant to play different parts of ourselves; taking action and executing a plan is part of living! We just need to have a balance between the three or it's easy to fall victim to all the drama.

Meditation has been my anchor, my anchor back to the space of the audience. When everything seems to be going wrong in our lives, or when we're caught up in a situation that feels so hard and endless, we can still have this distinction that everything will work out. There is a knowing that it's all unfolding in perfect order and that it's going to be okay; that *you* are going to be okay. Going within is my practice of coming back home.

Surrender To The Mystery

There is a tendency for us to try to grab onto certainty. It helps us feel secure and safe in an impulsive world that changes every day. But life is so unpredictable; we really never know what's going to happen next, no matter how much we plan. It helps to see the fun and challenge in this if you learn to let go of expectation.

If you ever feel like you just don't know what next step to take, and that there is "no light at the end" for you; or you're unsure of what life will have next for you: *Surrender to the Mystery*. Give up the need to be the one in charge. The more we push life, that harder life pushes back. Surrender to all possibilities of life, to the uncertainty – no matter how hard it is, and it *will* be hard (at first). I believe that life could be summed up into this little sentence: *Surrender to the glorious mystery*.

A Practice Of Surrendering

Lie on your bed, arms at your side, and legs straight. Begin to breathe softly into your belly. The lower abdomen should rise as you inhale and sink as you exhale. Let your breath be at its own speed and depth. It will naturally get slower and softer. Now start to let go. Feel your whole body sink more and more into your bed. Continue to surrender by relaxing every part of yourself - your eyes, your head, your feet, your arms, your neck and jaw, and your stomach. Let every contraction in your body open, soften and let go. It's amazing what you'll feel if you continue to do this over and over again. As we continue this exercise we can take it into our daily lives and when tension starts to rise up we can know what it's like to live from a space of surrender.

Some time ago I remember sitting in my doctor's office waiting for the double knock on the door. I was nervous as I was there for an MRI on my foot which was sporting an unsightly lump. (This might have been a bit of my own neurosis, but nevertheless I was scared.) The physician's assistant walked in and instantly exuded such a lovely presence. We got to talking; it was around the holidays so we were discussing gifts and what we were hoping from our loved ones. Then out of nowhere she said, "I believe expectations are premeditated resentments." I said, "Oh my – I love that." I wrote it down right away and am sharing it with you now. Isn't that powerful? This lit me up: *Expectations are premeditated resentments.* Here is what this means - we have expectations of people all the time, even when we don't think we do. Sometimes we don't realize it, but we have them for our families, our friends, our career, ourselves, you know – *the way things should be*. We expect people to treat us a certain way. We await respect, love, and kindness. But the reality is sometimes we just don't get that.

Having expectations of the people in our lives, whether hidden or known, causes resentment in the future. I can assure you that others will disappoint you – it will happen, time and time again. When we anticipate a certain action or response, our happiness is jeopardized and this can lead to bitterness. Because nine times out of ten it never goes the way we see it in our minds. No one wants this. It's easy to believe that we know how life is supposed to go; how people should act and what it is we want/need from them. Yet, as difficult as it may be, we have to be okay with what is. Our health and livelihood depend on it. This exercise can help us surrender ourselves to whatever may be.

"The truth lies in the question, not the answer."
Adyashanti

Questions to consider on meditation:

1. What is my relationship with silence?
2. What have I learned about meditation in the past?
3. Would I ever be willing to give it a try?

Questions on your current practices:

4. What makes *me* feel like I've been called back *home*?
5. In what ways do *I* experience silence already?
6. Can I afford *not* to start meditating?
7. Would I be willing to give up my image of "perfection" and simply do what I am able to do?

Questions for future growth:

8. What does the vision of all possibilities look like in my life? (What could it look like?)
9. What would I be willing to let go of and instead, embrace?
10. Who am I and what is it that I have come here to do?
11. Can I truly realize that I am a part of everything?

Change is constantly happening outside of our control. Our world will always be changing. The only way to ever find peace is to be okay with making adjustments and alterations along the way as you continue to grow and as the world fluctuates. This tool (meditation) will help you embrace the uncertain outcomes as they unfold. It'll help you ebb and flow with life and to embrace the depth and beauty of each moment.

Meditate. It's a practice - so just do it as much as you can, no matter what, and the benefits will come. But don't just do it for you – do it for the world. We can't solve our problems with the same small minds that created the problem; we need a shift in consciousness in order to see the solutions. Silence is the space where everything and anything becomes possible.

PART 6
Love Is The Source Of Everything

I realize that a lot of people instantly tighten at the word Love. Many of us are very careful about to whom we give it and express it, so a chapter on Love may cause some of you to close up and shut down a little (or a lot). Please know that I understand what it is like to retract from this word, as well. I also realize that Love is an extremely complex word and that I may only be touching the surface here, but I'm going for it. It's a topic I don't take lightly. I ask that you bear with me as I do my best to describe and promote such a powerful word.

The way I have broken down this chapter is in small sections and bite-sized pieces so that we may come to understand the many facets of Love – the tiny truths of Love that can alter our lives. I find it's easier for me and for others to learn about such a vast subject in this way.

What I know to be true is although many are afraid of Love, hide from Love, or fear being loved by others or loving others, we all have a relentless hunger for it in our lives. I believe we are constantly being drawn back to Love in subtle ways – whether we know it or can feel it.

Love is a force more formidable than any other. It is
invisible - it cannot be seen or measured; yet it is
powerful enough to transform you in a moment, and
offer you more joy than any material possession could.

-Barbara de Angelis

Where Do We Begin With Love?

The famous author Leo Buscaglia (known as Dr. Love in his time) was a professor at The University of Southern California; he taught in the Department of Special Education. He was a remarkable human being and his books have guided me for years. Buscaglia launched a "Love Class" for his students, and by no surprise was laughed at by the Board of Directors and his colleagues. This class was free of charge and conducted on his own time. After just one semester, there were 200 students on the waiting list for the next class. This experimental class sparked his best-selling book *Love,* in which he writes:

> "To live in Love is life's greatest challenge. It requires more subtlety, flexibility, sensitivity, understanding, acceptance, tolerance, knowledge and strength than any other human endeavor or emotion, for love and the actual world make up what seem like two great contradictory forces. On the other hand, man may know that only by being vulnerable can he truly offer and accept love."

We have all learned the concept of Love in different ways and forms. Some of you remember moments when you feel that love failed you, and destroyed you. Some of you can remember the exact time when you made your mind up about Love. Perhaps you went through a devastating breakup and from then on refused to ever open your heart again. And maybe for you, Love wasn't there when you were growing up. Feeling unloved and unworthy was a place of familiarity in my younger years; the agony and pain that comes with that is something no one ever wants to feel again.

As I have suggested numerous times in this book, please continue to stay open. I'm here with you, we're together, and none of us are alone. The reality is we all have different beliefs, different concepts and discoveries of Love. Perhaps we need to strip away everything we've ever known about Love to authentically experience the magnitude of its power.

My hope is that through this chapter we come to know a richer meaning of Love. My prayer is that we experience it at a far greater capacity than ever before. May we be strengthened, challenged and inspired to take this knowledge out into the world before us and create a change that will cause a shift on this planet. My one wish is that each one of us be the individual that gives and practices Love so greatly that we're never afraid to speak the words or display it in any moment.

Love Is The Underlying Source

Above all the noise and distractions, there resides Love. Past the incessant chatter inside of our minds, Love sits patiently waiting. Beyond our need to control and make sense of life, Love is welcoming us into the peace of mystery. When the world demands, Love invites. Where diversity resides, Love exudes alikeness and oneness. When you are stressed, Love breathes. Love is the underlying Source of everything.

I like to describe Love using analogies because when it is given a specific definition or put inside a box, its capabilities are belittled. Oceans are deep, wide and stretch farther than the eye can see – Love is the same. Like an ocean's tide, Love should overflow in our hearts spilling over into other people. It can be breathtaking when you witness an act of love. There is Love that is peaceful, magnificent, earth shattering, contagious, unfathomable, and effortless. There is Love in simple, easy, tiny acts of kindness and service – moments that seem so little, yet are incredibly powerful.

Sometimes Love is not always sunsets and rainbows. Believe me, the only Love I ever knew growing up was painful, hard, burdensome Love that shook my world to the core. An experience of Love can come with destructive storms; it can be hard, challenging and heart-wrenching. The storms come, and they come without warning. You lose someone you loved dearly, you suffer from a disease, or you lose a relationship you thought would last forever. I don't know why bad, unexplainable things like that happen, I truly don't. Like everything else, Love is a paradox – there are two sides to it. What I do know, though, is that God is Love and He can see things that we cannot. We were not made to understand, we were created to trust. There are some things we were just not meant to see in this season of our life. Sometimes, only a little light is shining, but it's all we may need at the time.

Here is a perspective I want you to ponder for a moment: What if everything we ever experience originates from Love? The moments when everything feels seamlessly unified, peaceful, serene, and even exciting. And the flashes of sadness, anger, hurt, despair. *What if living a fulfilled and meaningful life all boils down to moments of loving and being loved? (Or lack thereof?)*

Could it really be this simple? Love is simple, just not easy (hence the storms of life). The truth is that we human beings have different interpretations of Love. I encourage you to believe <u>your</u> truth, and to apply to your life what resonates with <u>your</u> soul. This is your life, and no one knows it better than you. I feel like I was born a person who always questioned the status quo; always felt as if things could go differently. I never followed "rules" exactly as they were taught, because I always believed there was more than one path to follow. I had a ceaseless drive to figure things out on my terms and to discover what life as a woman was about for me: not anyone else's version of how it should be.

However, I have learned qualities of Love through other people. I believe that is how we were designed, to lean on and learn from others. We are created to need others, to feed off of one another, and the connection we crave is there, all of the time.

I have always found that the most beautiful type of

Love is when one gives the other permission to shine their light the way *they* prefer, not the way we think they should. As Buscaglia writes,

> "Love needs freedom. Love is always free. It is both given and received freely, but it also needs freedom in order to grow. We cannot force others into our own way; we can only encourage them to find their own."

And so, hear my heart as I share with you, but only receive it if it is, in fact, aligned with how you choose to shine. When all else fails, if you have trouble letting go and can't embrace the silence, then please fall on Love. Love is the solid foundation where everything intertwines. That is who you are – a walking creation of Love.

Love Is Ageless

Love knows no age. All of my life I have befriended people of all ages, many more than 50 years my senior. People look at me with crazy eyes when I say, "Yes, my best friends are usually above the age of 50." No matter the age difference, I share an unexplainable connection with each one. I have always tried to be a person who sees the other *person* – not their appearance, their age, status, or anything else. And I have always felt at home speaking on topics such as spirituality, growth, Love, anger, hurt. I just could not bring myself to have another superficial, depthless conversation. I wanted to get to the heart of people; how they suffered, what they were passionate about, what lessons have they learned, how I could give to them and what I could gain from our friendship. That is how Love works; it sees a *soul* of someone, not their birth certificate. I am grateful to have discovered this at a young age, and because of this I have some of the best friendships on the planet. It is also because I have tried very hard for many years to remember: Stay open.

This is the same for you, too. Connection doesn't discriminate, or change, based upon how old or young you are. Have you ever had a beautiful interaction with someone much older or younger than you? It doesn't really matter, does it? In the midst of sharing Love back and forth with people, it's just there. It's just so beautifully expressed and received.

Aging is something that happens to our *bodies*. Our flesh and skin grow old, we get wrinkles, parts of us start to sag, and our hair turns different colors. Yet, our *soul* is ageless, our spirit inside of us doesn't know anything about aging. Our soul is still as fully alive and energized as it was in our youth. So Love must be the same way. There is no age on Love, it just is. Therefore, when sharing a connection with another there really aren't any criteria to meet for that to happen. It is what it is - Love. When it comes to Love and connection, time is meaningless and we all share in this invisible linking. Love is just Love.

Love Listens

I remember a time when I was having a really hard day; I felt stressed and exhausted. I came home to my sweetheart who instantly knew something was off. He grabbed a chair and pulled it right up next to me. "Talk to me honey. What's going on?" He sat with me and listened to me rant on and on about the tireless emotional problems I was having that day. True Love listens.

What I was yearning for at that moment was someone to listen. I just wanted someone to look at me, in all sincerity (at my worst), into my eyes, and simply listen. He saw my beauty without having to *try really hard* to see it.

Love should never be forced; it should be given and accepted easily. In fact, it's not really Love if it is forced.

It seems that in our technology-driven world today, it's difficult to get someone's *full* presence. If you want amazing relationships that are beyond your imagination, give your complete attention to the other; you'll start to see their entire being open up right before your eyes.

Love listens to people even when we completely disagree. We honor their opinions and beliefs because we, too, have our own. A dear friend always says, "Listening is the highest form of Love." It gives the other person acknowledgement that what they have to say truly matters. That's why, when someone comes to us with their heart open, it's so incredibly important that we give them the respect and attention they so deserve; that we take the time to shut down our laptops, turn off our phones and be totally present with them. (And who knows, it might also give you a break that you didn't know you needed!)

Love Gives

It's easy to take a look around our world, and in our personal lives, and see scarcity – or deficiency. With all of the hardships and suffering taking place, it can seem like there isn't enough to go around – not enough resources, time, money, food, water, etc. Love, however, is an endless supply that we can always give. Love is something that you can continually give and never run out of.

When we give to others, expectations usually follow. We expect a gift back, another kind word in return, heck – even a thank you would suffice. Authentic Love gives without expecting anything in return. Where one would see lack, Love sees abundance. There is so much to give and you never lose when it comes to Love.

Love is an endless sea that you can continually call upon to give you strength and that others need so desperately. Remember, what you give out always comes back. The seeds of Love that you plant *will* show up in your life when you least expect it. You don't lose anything when you Love, you only gain; your benefit comes from within, not from other people. When you give with Love, something inside of you changes, it transforms you. So never be afraid to give Love, even to those who cannot seem to appreciate it or notice it at the time.

Love Is Born From The Inside

The day we are born is the start of our souls longing for unconditional Love. We are always ready for it, however at times it may be hard to muster up the courage to accept it as it comes. It takes incredible bravery to Love fully and deeply, but even more courage to receive it.

Some of us cannot find the Love that is inside of our hearts for ourselves, so we search the outer world for it. We mistakenly believe that when we land that great job, get that promotion, buy that new car, and have that house or relationship, that we will somehow feel whole. Wanting and desiring those kinds of material things is not wrong; in fact, having high standards for your life is an admirable thing. Yet, when so much energy is invested in attaining those things to feel complete, you have entered a race you will never win.

Love is born from the inside out, not the outside in. The truth is that Love never goes away. It is always within us at any given moment, and available to tap into. Some replace that feeling with so many perishables that they are left feeling worthless, unimportant and undeserving. *We can always turn inward to Love, at all times.* In the midst of an argument or disagreement, Love is there, waiting for you to recognize it. Love is there when you feel stuck, doubtful or unworthy; waiting for you to pay attention to it, waiting for you to see beyond the small problem and see a greater picture.

Instead of relearning Love, we need to simply strip away all the misconceptions we already have of it. In this moment you are a creature of Love. You breathe Love, you exude Love, every decision you make in your life is based upon the level of Love you have in your heart. We can always change our minds about Love. We can change our stories we have created around the word.

One of my favorite sayings is a very simple one by Gandhi, "Where there is Love, there is life." If you are breathing right now that means you are flowing in and out Love.

Love Laughs

Where have we gone wrong? It seems people in our society take themselves so seriously that they forget to laugh anymore. When was the last time you had a deep belly laugh and felt the feeling to your core? It sometimes appears as if our culture has lost its sense of spontaneity. If things don't go according to plan, we can't handle it. Be sporadic, change a plan, go along with an idea that seems crazy – do it, it'll bring you back to what is real. Some of us were raised that we should be seen and not heard, so when we find something funny we may chuckle a bit, but still remain reserved.

Laugh, my darling, laugh! Don't be afraid to *laugh out loud*. The light that illuminates and radiates from laughter is so beautiful. And boy, is it contagious. We have to be childlike again; embrace the wide-eyed-wonder look back into our lives. If someone says something funny – laugh. Or laugh at yourself; you know how silly we are as humans? If you look, it won't be hard to find. Ultimately, you are giving a great gift to others and yourself. A day without laughter is a day wasted. At the center of laughter you will find Love.

Love *Is* Tangible

People have a hard time trusting something that cannot be seen or touched. Enter in: Faith. Love falls into this category. But, can you recall a time you have experienced that rush of Love, that one moment in your life when you surely have *felt* Love?

How can something that cannot be touched seem so real?

Consider this. At a wedding ceremony, finally the moment has arrived when the bride is walking down the aisle after hours of making sure she exudes perfection. Every set of eyes are upon her while the music is playing softly in the background. But then, one person glances back at the groom to see his face bursting with a light and a glow that is indescribable. The man (or partner) has this look upon his or her face of knowing that if all the certainty and hope in his lifetime were to be bottled up into one moment - this is it.

That's Love reflecting back and forth into the eyes of the couple, and everyone in the room can feel it. Some even have chills. Only the two are getting married, yet the room is full of tears, of awe, of wonder in the beauty of their Love. It fills the air, something that isn't "tangible" in that moment feels almost as if you could reach your hand out and touch it, it seems that real.

It doesn't have to take a wedding to feel that type of deep-rooted Love. Love is so very real; we can touch it with our hearts. Why would a perfect stranger reach out and help another? I once coached a Dale Carnegie course customized for a group in the inner city of Detroit. These teenagers were seeking to become successful young adults. For some, this would be their only taste of an education.

The stories that I listened to in that class were unreal to me. Young adolescents were pouring out their hearts to my colleague and me. Many of these kids had experienced things you and I don't even want to imagine – parents robbed or murdered, drug addictions, suicide attempts, harming others. I had never heard anything like it.

Still these kids had hopes, dreams, and visions of becoming doctors, the world's best lawyers, and teachers. This program had given them hope. *That, to me, is making Love real.*

During a "Breakthrough Barriers" session, the teens were asked to share their past hurts – their deepest burdens that they had been dying to share their entire lives. It was an extremely emotional time in my life and I was affected deeply by what happened next. One of the girls was so overwhelmed by the pain that she ran out of the room gasping for air. I followed her into the bathroom and found three other girls in there crying … perhaps they were tears of disappointment, discouragement, doubt, pain, abandonment, hate, rage or bitterness. In that moment, I knew I could be an instrument of Love and shed some light on this dark, yet healing, time.

One of the young ladies ran into my arms, sobbing uncontrollably, telling me how unloved and screwed up she felt. In this moment everything seemed to disappear for me – all my troubles, my hurts, MY pains, all vanished in this second.

As tears started to roll down my cheeks, I thought a silent prayer and began whispering in her ear, **I love you, I accept you, I see you, and it's going to be okay.**

The more I said it, the more I felt her breath start to slow down. I felt the deepest sigh of relief coming from her soul. In that moment, I had yet again realized the power of Love. The power of someone, anyone, hearing your heart. That is when I realized, beyond a shadow of a doubt, that Love is absolutely tangible. I learned that simply putting yourself in another's shoes can be incredibly powerful and something people don't do often. Empathy is an act of Love. When someone comes to you for help, how do you respond? Can you recall a time when someone came to you in an authentic moment of desperation? How did you react?

What Does The World Know About Love?

I know that the world can be filled with what seems to be darkness. There is crime, murder, grief, and disappointment. The media is not afraid to give the negative news. If we look, we can always find something wrong and something to be afraid of. Our world can be very fear-based. It seems that our world has distorted the image of Love. Some people are so buried in darkness that they forget light even exists. They forget how powerful light can be, even more so than darkness. Love isn't spoken in our societies often enough; it is not reinforced as the Source of life.

It's possible to see light in our world. It's possible to be activists for Love. Love is natural. Love is effortless. Love doesn't withdraw. Even in the midst of heartache and sadness, Love resides there, too. When we fix our eyes on Love, we can find it in the most unusual places. We find it in our everyday activities. When someone opens a door for another, that is an act of Love. When a person smiles at a stranger, that is Love, too. When you give someone your full presence when they're speaking to you, Love is present.

When a person completely forgets about their needs in order to help another human being, that is Love. And the ability to say no to people in order to take care of yourself is Love; Loving yourself.

Do not conform to what the world will tell you about Love. Don't let the world fool you into thinking Love doesn't exist anymore. It surely does. It exists in laughter, in a new day, in the eyes of another; Love can be present in anything.

Matthew 7:7 says, "Ask and it will be given to you; seek and you will find; knock and the door will be opened to you." Isn't this true for life? When we seek Love in any situation, we will surely find it. When we seek the good in our world and the opportunities within, they will be there, waiting for us to meet them head on.

Try to find Love today; look for it in every situation. What do I admire about this person? What do I see about who they are? In an issue you may be facing, where is there Love? You will find it, when you seek with all of your heart.

You Can Give Love,
When You Are Connected To Love

"You cannot give away what you don't already have." Have you heard this expression before? Maybe you have heard in it passing, or it's so cliché to you that you've missed the meaning. Or maybe you never heard it before. I find this idea to be very true, think about it; you cannot possibly give another person anything without first having it yourself. So why would Love be any different?

May I suggest a new perspective? You can give Love when you are connected to Love. Notice how I say "connected." In order to *have* something it insinuates that you first have to *get*. Love doesn't work like that. You never have to *get* Love. Love is always inside of us. We are born of Love and it resides within, therefore it is a feeling and an expression that never leaves us.

However, we can wander away from Love. I have done it a billion times, and so has every human on the planet. It's just in our DNA to drift away from Love from time to time; examples include unhappiness, guilt, worry, fear, anxiety, doubt, anger, negativity, jealousy. All of those emotions keep us from Love.

Isn't it great, though, to have the comfort of knowing that Love never leaves us and that we can call on it at any time? When other emotions arise it takes awareness to draw us back to Love. That is why meditation is so essential to our lives — it roots us back to Love. And when we experience emotions that we don't like, we have a tool to use to return to Love.

Stay connected and everything else will flow. Nothing is ever wrong when you make decisions out of Love. Do not spend your life searching for something you don't have to find. Some people try so hard to "find" Love that they miss it. I think the hardest part is not to fight to get it back, but to simply recognize when to return back to it.

Love Without Labels

When I take a moment and quiet my mind, I can quickly notice the thoughts that I am thinking. My thoughts are not me, I am not my thoughts, but they seem so real. If I really take a step back I hear it: "Oh wow, that's pretty." "No, I don't like that, it's ugly." "I am short." "I don't like this shirt on me." "This food is great." This is what I call labeling. Labels are not right or wrong, good or bad, it is simply classifying our thoughts into certain categories. Even if the words we are speaking *look* true, and *seem* to be true, they're simply our own descriptions. In his book, *Love,* Leo Buscaglia passionately suggests,

> "Labels are distancing phenomena. They push us away from each other. Black men. What's a black man? I've never known two alike. Does he love? Does he care? What about his kids? Has he cried? Is he lonely? Is he beautiful? Is he happy? Is he giving something to someone? These are the important things."

Think high school. No matter what generation you are, we all had cliques; jocks, nerds, cheerleaders, band geeks, you name it. And it doesn't stop there, it trickles over into college. Your major might determine what "group" you are a part of. And it definitely doesn't stop there either; in our professional lives we have bosses, coworkers and different generations. Labels exist. Labels are not always bad, sometimes they are necessary. But not when it comes to Love. So often we don't Love because we see separateness among each other. We see divisions and differences, we see right and we see wrong. Love sees only one. Love sees oneness among all things. What if we could see that each one of us struggles? If you think of it this way, doesn't every person crave connection and understanding?

Love Is In The Details

Let's say you haven't had a magnificent experience with Love; perhaps it's not been as heart-racing or earth-shattering as you want, or as you believe it should be. Don't worry, and don't think for one second that your tiny moments of happiness, generosity or inspiration are not important. It all matters.

What if it all counts? I think our younger generation has a distinctive "emergency-like" feeling to be successful. Everyone is competing for *their* moment, for *their* work to be noticed. And unless you are a famous writer, actor, entrepreneur, etc., then you just haven't "made it." But, what about the small acts of kindness and success that we don't hear about? For example, those people who are taking care of their sick parents or kids. What constitutes success, anyway? What if the smallest act of Love counts? Consider that it all counts. Love can be exhibited in the details. The times that no one notices can be the most impactful to the world.

The "High Road" And The "Other Way"

In every moment we are constantly being challenged to take the "high road" when we really want to act out on whatever emotion arises. For example, if someone hurts us we automatically become quick to defend ourselves and want to tell them all the ways that they are wrong. But then Love kicks in, our higher Self that says to us, "There's a better way to treat this person. Remember kindness, mercy, and compassion?"

It is human nature to want to ride the wave that emotion creates, but if we are searching for true spiritual growth, that won't get us there. In those moments of tension and stress we must ask, "What's the best way I can respond right now?," "What would help me to grow?" Taking the high road is not so easy, especially if we are caught in a state of impatience and irritation. Some moments we just want to forget all about the "high road" and withdraw. But, if we can continue to at least try to do better each day, our lives will be anything but boring and miracles will unfold before our eyes.

Love Has Boundaries

Do you remember what I've asked of you from the beginning of this book? Just to remind you, I have asked you to remain open to what comes your way – but especially open to Love. However, when it comes to loving, there is something you must truly understand. When you Love others and give all that you possibly can, some people will take advantage of your unconditional Love. They will see you for who you are – a giver. And they will take. They will take your time, your energy, your resources, and your attention. Be on guard because Love can only be given openly when you come from a place of abundance, not of desperation.

It is okay to set boundaries when it comes to Love. Some people in your life should be loved from a safe distance. The truth is we can continually send Love to people, even if we aren't in close proximity to them. Right now, wherever you are, I can send Love to you. Love is an energy that expands farther than we can possibly fully understand. It's a force within us that can move mountains and change lives. You have to remember to keep that part within your heart safe from the negative opinions of others. Safeguard your heart because it is sensitive and vulnerable to those who can hurt it.

You do not lack the capability to Love by setting boundaries. On the contrary, it is simply another way to Love that person. You can choose not to spend your time with someone and still Love them. Being mistreated at the expense of your well-being is not Love, its abuse. It's imperative that we stand up for ourselves and protect our spirit that is free, giving and loving.

Love Is Overwhelming

Love is absolutely overwhelming. When you experience Love it can seem uncomfortable and terrifying because of it's incredible power. At times, overpowering feelings of joy can seem hard to handle. Almost as if you could explode right out of your body because in those moments your consciousness is expanding. You are out of the relative; time disappears, nagging issues you've been facing seem to wash away.

On the other hand, if someone is showering their Love upon you – it can seem as if it is too much. In both situations I have come to the understanding to *just be with it.* To be still and do my best to feel deeply and receive what is going on within me.

Love is also unbelievably hard. I have found that it does not get easier to show Love in spite of another's wrongdoing. It does not get easier to choose Love when you've been hurt very badly. It does not get easier to walk this earth with an open heart. Sometimes, it's even hard for me to express my joy to others that may not understand it. But I would rather walk in Love than to experience the tremendous amount of pain that comes with being closed off from it.

You see, pain is inevitable no matter which way you choose, we can't escape pain. Though, with Love comes an incredible amount of fulfillment and adventure. It will never steer you in the wrong direction. In your moments of overwhelm, the more you can practice noticing what is going on inside of you and accept it fully, the more you can experience the joy and wonder that Love offers.

You Matter, They Matter, It All Matters

Some of us place great importance on acquiring things/possessions/relationships, but when we finally attain them the feeling of need goes away. We don't want them anymore; they have become stale and we have no more passion or excitement for them.

I remember being on a beautiful beach in Hawaii. White sand glistened under my bare feet as I gazed at the sunset over a never-ending ocean. The tide was light that night and the soft water caressed my feet and ankles. Each time the water drew back, I could feel a light breeze gently brush against my cheek and through my hair. Taking a deep breath in, noticing the silence and beauty, I thought, "Is this what Love feels like? Is this what it smells like? Is this what Love looks like?"

As I sat down in the sand I could feel goose bumps run all up and down my body, feeling grateful to be there. I rested there, witnessing the wonder of the earth and breathing in all the magnificence of my last evening in paradise. If this is what love is like, I didn't want to leave. I wanted to stay right in that place, forever. I wanted to bask in the feeling of complete freedom, joy, peace and love, forever. The feeling was completely overwhelming, as I am sure you have felt before. You know the feeling of pure bliss; they tend to come in moments: The moment you hold your first child, the moment you've seen something come to fruition that you've longed for, or the moment of looking into the eyes of someone you love. Maybe you are familiar with what I'm describing, maybe you've never felt this way before, or perhaps you have a vague memory of feeling this way a very long time ago.

You may know these moments very well, so when they are not present you feel empty, a void, or like you need to **do** something to make it come back. It's like a new job, we get so excited on the first day; it's a new challenge, new change, new people, new chapter, you're on cloud nine ... fast forward months later and you would give *anything* to be able to quit your job.

Whatever "beach" *you* are on, whatever sun is setting for you, wherever you are at this point in your life - it *all* matters, every part of it is being used for a purpose. Often times, we must **choose** Love. It has to be a continuous decision. Trust life, it knows what it's doing.

Love Always Creates,
But What Are You Creating?

In all moments we are creating. There is no such thing as a specifically creative person because each one of us continuously creates. We either make joy for others and ourselves, or we create suffering, doubt and pain. Each action that we take has a reaction that is a lot more powerful than some of us realize.

What are you creating? When you leave someone's presence, how do you think they feel? Do you make people feel hopeful, relaxed, and encouraged? Or do your actions produce a fearful and negative environment? Every word we speak plants an emotion into another person. I'm not saying that there will never be problems and that we should never experience pain, but we need to have an awareness of our effect on people. We are always creating – so what do you create? Do you play? Do you play with life or fear life? Do you play with your creativity or avoid it? Are you open to new ideas or do you judge that which comes your way?

There is a beautiful book entitled, *Comfortable With Uncertainty* that has touched my life profoundly. It's authored by Pema Chodron, an American Buddhist nun and renowned Tibetan meditation master. In that book she shares this powerful story,

"A big, burly samurai comes to a Zen master and says, 'Tell me the nature of heaven and hell.'

The Zen master looks him in the face and says, 'Why should I tell a scruffy, disgusting, miserable slob like you? A worm like you, do you think I should tell you anything?'

Consumed by rage, the samurai draws his sword and raises it to cut off the master's head.

The Zen master then says, 'That's hell.'

Instantly, the samurai understands that he has just created his own hell - black and hot, filled with hatred, self-protection, anger and resentment. He sees that he was so deep in hell he was ready to kill someone. Tears fill up his eyes as he puts his palms together to bow in gratitude for this insight.

The Zen master says, 'That's heaven.'

This view is no 'Hell is bad and heaven is good' or 'Get rid of hell and just seek heaven.' Instead, we encourage ourselves to develop an open heart and an open mind to heaven, to hell, to everything. Only with this kind of equanimity can we realize that no matter what comes along, we're always standing in the middle of a sacred space. Only with equanimity can we see that everything that comes into our circle has come to teach us what we need to know."

This taught me a great lesson that we are always creating and most magnificent thing about this is that we have the power to choose. We are called in every moment to choose whether we want to create a heaven or a hell for us or for those around us.

Love Starts With A Single Desire

Love is complex and can seem scary, but it's *essential*. There are so many other qualities of Love to explore, it simply starts with the desire to want to. Love is our vehicle to becoming our highest Self possible. You don't need to have all the answers. You don't need to be perfect. You're not broken and don't need to be fixed. All you need is the desire to start; Love starts with a single desire that we all possess. It's about recognizing this desire and continually cultivating it in your life.

Be patient and easy on yourself, you really are doing the best you can. When it comes to helping other people, never give up. When it comes to the person you're in love with, never give up (or discern when it is time to let go as that in and of itself is Love). When it comes to your deepest desires and dreams, never give up on them. However, when it comes to your suffering, give it up. When it comes to pleasing every human being in your life, give it up. When it comes to trying so hard to get someone to love you, give it up. When it comes to your precious Self, however, never ever give up. No one else on this earth will cherish, take care of, and love you the way that you can. Be easy on yourself. You're not broken, but if you feel you are, embrace brokenness. *Because we are all a beautiful masterpiece of creation and deserve to be here.* We deserve a life without suffering and a life that we truly love.

Therefore, allow mistakes to happen. Allow the bumps and bruises to show up. Allow yourself to make weight loss goals and totally mess up by day three. Accept that you will say the wrong thing at the wrong time – time and time again. Embrace the imperfections because that is where your light can really shine. Then get back up on the horse and try again. Never stop trying to be better than you used to be. We can *only* grow from a place of Love, not a place of "fixing" ourselves. Stop chasing what you already possess. You already possess greatness, truth, and inner peace. You do. Stand tall and delighted because you deserve to be here; never give up on yourself, okay?

The Source Is All-Inclusive

When we realize that we are all one and come from the same Source, there is a deep peace that transcends our understanding. We come to the conclusion that there is nothing separate from ourselves. There is no division and the Source excludes *no one*. God has no requirements for His Love. If anything or anyone tells you differently, it's simply not true.

We relax in the truth that we're always being taken care of by an intelligence that is greater than our own. I'd encourage you to notice the synchronicities that line up in your life and see that it's all on purpose and apart of a bigger picture than what we can see with our eyes. You need not worry of the future and instead focus on the certainty that comes with living in each present moment just as it is.

Know that you have the unlimited power of the Source inside of you. It is available in each moment, you need only to be still. Ask for help. We were not meant to live in the physical world alone, we need help. Don't be afraid to ask for it and trust that the infinite Source will guide you to the right person, place, and you will have everything you will ever need.

Inner Peace

Inner peace doesn't mean that you sit still in the world and be cautious of every little thing you say and do. It doesn't mean that you are aloof and lack caring for other people's suffering. It also doesn't mean that we live flat lined and with one level of emotion. It means that from a centered, grounded, and unshakable knowing everything else can emerge. From this strong awakening of who we really are and the power we possess within comes: Joy, gratitude, happiness, excitement, courage, wonder, and intensified fulfillment.

If you're thinking to yourself, "I don't yearn for peace. Or at least I never thought I did," I get it. Sometimes it's not the first thing we think of when we are inquiring about our lives. However I can assure you that all that we long for can be manifested into our lives with a relaxation and peace that it's on it's way. The lives we deeply want can only come from a trust that cannot be shaken from any external source. That's inner peace.

What Is The Meaning Of Life?

Technically, this question is for you to answer for yourself. The purpose of your life is sacred and something you can discover in your own time. Still, I'd like to share the guiding truths that have been my anchor to realizing the deepest meaning of my life.

Death is inevitable and comes without warning to all of us. So what is the purpose of living? Doesn't it just make sense to stay comfortable, live in the realms of familiarity, raise our kids and just stay quiet? What really is the commitment of being courageous, strong or vulnerable, when we know we are going to die? What is the point of it all?

Why do we care to "leave a legacy," or to keep working on the betterment of ourselves? Here's why: Because after you pass on, there will be others on this planet that are still living. People that have a chance to make a difference in the lives of the ones they see every day… human beings that still have a chance to change the world on a big level. YOUR job, OUR job, MY job is to give all that we can to those that we can while we are here. It is our duty and privilege to love others - truly love people for who they are. By doing the very best that we can at every moment, our existence just may be contributing to the positive change of another human being.

That's why. That's what life is all about. It's about living up to our full potential ... it's about never giving up on ourselves because the people that are here need us. *We* need us. And before we are gone, we want to know deep within our hearts that we have done everything we can and have **given everything we have to those who are still living.** The souls you impact on earth in the physical world will continue to live on forever. If this is the case, then is death even final? Love is eternal; Love never ends. When we Love one another with our entire being it lives on forever.

There's a popular saying that we have one life that should be lived to the fullest because once you're gone, you're done. Yes, we need to live a full life, but it's more than that: Depending upon the level of commitment and Love you pour into others while you are alive, *you can continue to make positive changes in the world even after your death.*

If you seek the highest truth – and if you search with all your heart for the Source – you'll connect to it. If everything in you wants a peaceful life, if you have a burning desire to learn from your suffering and become your highest Self, you *will*. You absolutely will attain genuine power and inner peace. This process, however, is not instantaneous; we will always be changing, learning and growing. Remember that inner peace is a moment-by-moment practice and the simple awareness of your breath can bring you back to the Source and allow you to hear your inner voice prominently.

To recognize your capacity to Love, and to open your heart to all that Love encompasses, will allow you to undergo any change, uncertainty or alteration in your life. You'll come to the realization that Love is you and you are Love; that it's the one, true, and only Source.

You're now prepared to live one day at a time with eyes that see the whole of who you are, that see all possibilities, and the truth. My greatest desire is that you live up to your highest Self expression possible. So one day when it's time to change forms and death comes knocking at your door you can look back and confidently say, *"I did this. I did this thing called life and I am at peace with who I am and what I have created for others."*

ABOUT THE AUTHOR

Hailey Jordan Yatros is a sought-after Inspirational Speaker, Coach, Next-Generation Thought Leader and Author of the book *The Millennial Makeover*, which has sold thousands of copies worldwide. Hailey's work has inspired people from all walks of life live a more meaningful and conscious life. She has been featured in HayHouse Radio, Tiny Buddha, Elite Daily, Vice Magazine, Thought Catalog, MetroParent Magazine, Millennial Magazine and many more. Connect with Hailey on Facebook to learn more about how you can work with her and the details of her upcoming national television show.

Dear Reader,

My journey has been messy, every bit of it. Whose hasn't? It's not been easy to get to where I am today, that's for sure. However, it has been and continues to be worth every heartache, obstacle, and painful moment. I'd rather do things afraid than not do things *because* I am afraid. From publishing a book before I could order my first legal drink, to coaching thousands of people by the time I was 23 years old, one core internal belief has guided my life: Nothing is impossible for me. Which also means, there is nothing impossible for you, either.

As a child of God, there is nothing I cannot do; this type of faith has landed me in the most amazing and the most frightening places. For me, writing has been a practice of coming back home; a place where I feel I can share my greatest treasures with others. In the process, I have been able to help my readers from all over the world live with the same inner confidence.

My hope is that you'll continue to stay connected with me and keep the conversation on peace alive by sharing with your friends and passing this book along. What inspired you while reading? What projects are you now taking on? What challenged you or enabled growth? I want to learn all about you! Please let me know via Facebook, email or other social sites – you can even send me pictures of your beautiful faces, too!

I am incredibly grateful for you, and this precious life we've been given … and guess what? It's only the beginning.

All my Love,
Hailey

Twitter: @HaileyYatros
Facebook: Hailey Jordan Yatros
For all inquiries contact: info@haileyyatros.com or visit www.haileyyatros.com

ACKNOWLEDGEMENTS

I am deeply grateful for so many people, it's hard to know where to start. Thank you to the following people for your relentless encouragement and presence in my life: Daniel, Larry and Jo Kelley, my Mom and Dad, Susan Maloney, my big wonderful family, Sandy Richards, Sarah Carr, Susan Dooley, Amanda Rivera, Kay Beech, Susie Dahlmann, Greg Long, and Denise Brooks.

I want to thank my amazing editor, Laura McMurry. Your insights and suggestions made this book complete. Also to my beautiful friend Susan Willnus for collaborating with me on the meditation chapter; your wisdom and life experiences greatly impacted the evolution of this book.

Lastly, I want to whole-heartedly thank my online community and support system. I love each of you so much and so admire your bravery, openness, and willingness to share your truth and grow yourself to the highest level possible. We really are all in this together.

28016986R00093

Made in the USA
Columbia, SC
09 October 2018